SEMEIA 58

DISCURSIVE FORMATIONS, ASCETIC PIETY AND THE INTERPRETATION OF EARLY CHRISTIAN LITERATURE, PART 2

Editor:
Vincent L. Wimbush

©1992
by the Society of Biblical Literature

Published by
SCHOLARS PRESS
P.O. BOX 15399
Atlanta, GA 30333-0399

Printed in the United States of America
on acid free paper

CONTENTS

PART 2

Preface v

Contributors to This Issue vii

III

9. Translocation of Parental Images in Fourth–Century Ascetic Texts: Motifs and Techniques of Identity
   Marilyn Nagy 3

10. Through a Glass Darkly: Diverse Images of the APOTAKTIKOI(AI) of Early Egyptian Monasticism
    James E. Goehring 25

11. Demons and the Perfecting of the Monk's Body: Monastic Anthropology, Daemonology and Asceticism
    Richard Valantasis 47

12. Ascetic Behavior and Color-ful Language: Stories about Ethiopian Moses
    Vincent L. Wimbush 81

IV

13. Ascesis, Authority and Text: *The Acts of the Council of Saragossa*
    Virginia Burrus 95

14. Regimen for Salvation: Medical Models in Manichaean Asceticism
    Jason David BeDuhn 109

Response: Old Water in New Bottles: The Contemporary Prospects for the Study of Asceticism
    Geoffrey Galt Harpham 135

Glossary 149

Selected Bibliography: Asceticism and Discursive Strategies 153

PREFACE

This is the second of the two volume collection of essays that attempt to identify and account for the discursive strategies and rhetorics used to describe, enjoin, inveigh against or generally problematize forms of renunciation in selected religious literatures of Greco-Roman antiquity. Included in this volume is a provocative essay by well-known literary critic Geoffrey Harpham, author of *The Ascetic Imperative in Culture and Criticism* (1987). It forms a general response to the whole collection of essays found in Part 1 (*Semeia* 57) and Part 2 (*Semeia* 58).

                                        Vincent L. Wimbush
                                        Editor

CONTRIBUTORS TO THIS ISSUE

Jason BeDuhn
  Indiana University
  Bloomington IN

Virginia Burrus
  Drew University
  Madison NJ

James E. Goehring
  Mary Washington College
  Fredricksburg VA

Geoffrey Galt Harpham
  Tulane University
  New Orleans LA

Verna E. F. Harrison
  Berkeley CA

Marilyn Nagy
  Palo Alto CA

Richard Valantasis
  St. Louis University
  St. Louis MO

Vincent L. Wimbush
  Union Theological Seminary
  New York City

III

Translocation of Parental Images in Fourth–Century Ascetic Texts: Motifs and Techniques of Identity

Marilyn Nagy
Palo Alto CA

ABSTRACT

Recent work in object relations theory and in anthropological culture theory offers perspectives with which to see the fourth–century ascetic enterprise as a deeply ethical attempt on the part of ascetic practitioners to achieve a counter-cultural identity exhibiting the high values of the culture. The cases of Anthony, Pachomius, Theodore and Ammon, who sharply cut off all contact and memory of family and home at the onset of their ascetic vocations, are studied as a program in which the ascetic replicated the identity of the martyrs in their relation to the culture as a whole.

This paper is a thank offering to the Ascetic Behavior in Greco-Roman Antiquity Group, which for a number of years has generously allowed me as an interdisciplinarian to participate in and to learn from their ongoing work. In the paper, I attempt to understand feelings of affinity and affection for the Christian ascetic heroes of the fourth century and beyond by examining a particular motif which appears with striking vitality at the apex of the first great movement to the desert in Egypt. My questions are about identity, how it develops, what a "self" is, and what it might mean to have a counter-cultural identity.

My aim is not to reduce religious inquiry to psychological terms; my primary interests are ethical, and my sense of "true" religion has largely to do with value experiences.

Certain areas of psychology are coming close to hard science in their understanding of the nature of the human being. If present theories continue to be validated—and I think that a variety of inquiries coming from physiological, experimental and clinical branches of psychology are now converging in some commonly held convictions about the conditions for human development—we may be able to anchor ethical beliefs in biological fact. There are vast implications here for understanding religious experience, and for being able to affirm the "truth" value of the ascetic's path to salvation and his or her claim to have found God, in terms which are comprehensible in our own cultural situation. There are however many things that are not yet known, and may never be known, about the proportionate role of culture and phylogenetic hard wiring in the human person in the development of identity. I can offer therefore only some current considerations.

When Anthony, who had spent his early years quietly at home, desiring neither schooling nor friends of his own age, was puzzling after his parents' death what to do with his life, it came to him that he ought not to cling to his home nor to the security of his inheritance, but should seek a new home altogether. From then on he determined not to "look back on things of his parents, nor call his relatives to memory" (Athanasius, 1980: chap. 3, 32).[1] And if in future he should indeed call to mind his old home and its comforts, or his sister in the place where she now lived among the virgins of his village, or any of the relatives with whom he used to feel close, then it was only the devil crashing around and making noise in the night—a devil who would if possible keep him from the good and destroy his salvation (Athanasius, 1980: chap. 5, 45).

At a crucial point in the Bohairic Life of Pachomius (if the text is set up in dramatic form it is indeed the turning point of the story, when the trials of childhood and youth and the years of preparatory training result in the founding of the monastery at Tabennesi), three suppliants apply to become monks. Pachomius tests their vocation before admitting them, and there is just one question: can you renounce your parents and follow the Savior? (Veilleux: 1.23, 45)[2]

Pachomius' pupil and spiritual son Theodore ran away from home as a child in order to become a monk, and when his mother came looking for him he refused to see her, citing the Gospel command. That Theodore's younger brother, Paphnouti, when he and his mother stood on the rooftop in order to at least glimpse Theodore on his way to work, should then run after Theodore calling out that he too wanted to become a monk, marks the total abnegation of parents as a thrilling, heroic act in the culture of that time and place (Goehring, 1990:350ff.).

The Letter of Ammon, too, records that his parents had scoured the monasteries throughout Egypt to find their lost son before giving him up for dead (Goehring, 1986:178f.).[3] It must not have been so uncommon that sons left their parents without permission. At least in the fourth century, and at least in the types of ascetic endeavor which characterized the move to the outer desert in Egyptian and near Egyptian lands, rejection of parents and home was more absolute than anything that had occurred in earlier periods.

Although several passages in the New Testament command the loosening of bonds between parents and children in order to follow Christ,[4] there is some evidence that Christians had difficulty reconciling the most severe of these commands, especially Luke 14:26, which requires the

Christian actually to hate father, mother, wife and children, with the contradictory and equally clear Biblical commandment to honor one's parents. Clement of Alexandria claimed that the docetist heretic Julius Cassian had misinterpreted the passage completely when he quoted it to prove the sinfulness of marriage. "This is not a command to hate one's family," wrote Clement. It means only that one should not give in to irrational impulses, and one's family should be focused on bearing fruit for the Lord rather than absorbed in the customs and politics of the city (Clement, 1954:3.15.97, p. 85f.). In another discussion, Clement explains how the true gnostic understands the saying about hating one's father and mother. It is because he stands above any dependency or support which might come to his own flesh by reason of the family connection. Instead, the gnostic loves his kinfolk by giving "his own good things to those whom he holds dearest" (Clement, 1954:7.12.79–80, p. 144). The Christian is to live life *as though* a stranger and a pilgrim—there is to be a loosening of bonds—but there is no talk of *actual* departure from the city, nor of abandonment of family and friends, for the Christian gnostic has a mission among them of bringing them to a higher truth, and of bearing their burdens.

Only Origen, preaching martyrdom to Ambrose, urges him quite literally to learn to hate his wife and children, brothers and sisters—to hate his own soul in this world—so that he can become a true disciple of Jesus and preserve his soul for everlasting life (Origen: chap. 37, 420). Even so, Origen does not neglect to add that Ambrose can actually assist his children more effectively as a saint in heaven, praying for them now with greater knowledge and understanding than if he had remained with them in the world.

The notion that the path to salvation means total rejection of parents and family did not, even by the end of the fourth century, seem to have caught on as much in the Eastern areas of the Church as it did in the Egyptian desert. Writing about 386, John Chrysostom urges parents not to stand in the way of their sons' vocations. Not having chosen the path toward power and high office, the son will never compete with his father for honor, but will love him all the more, "not only because of the law of nature, but above all because of God for whose sake he has come to despise all other things" (John Chrysostom: 2.9, p. 115). Besides, if the parents miss the company of their children overly much, they can always walk (to the monastery, just outside the city) to visit and talk with them, and thus be gladdened not only by the sight of their children but also by the receiving of the greatest philosophical fruits from them (2.18, p. 168). The great Cappadocians Gregory, Basil, Macrina, Peter and Naucratius, together with their mother, made monastic life into a family enterprise, sharing both their honors and their losses, so that their bonds with each other became indistinguishable from their fervor for the divine. Gregory is proud to report his unrestrained tears, as well as those of the entire populace, at the death of his sister Macrina. He attends to her body himself and arranges the details of her great funeral, so as "not to leave undone anything suitable for such an occasion."

But it is John Cassian, of all those who drew inspiration from the desert fathers of Egypt, who has Abbot Abraham in the twenty-fourth Conference take the difficult text of Luke 14:26 at its full value. You may leave your family and go on a pilgrimage in the flesh, he said, but until you have endured the separation with your heart, and have given up every memory of those in your past, you have not understood the principle of renunciation, nor the main reason for a life of solitude in the desert. Not until you no longer feel either joy or sorrow at the fortunes and misfortunes of family members can you feel safe that your exertions will receive their due reward (John Cassian: 24.2.11, pp. 532, 536f.). You should not allow others, and especially not parents, to supply physical necessities of food and shelter in a retreat near home, be it ever so available and peaceful, because to live by their charity drags you down to earthly things and keeps you in a state of dependence.

1. Object Relations Approaches to Identity

This point, about the necessity of a total loosening of affectional bonds with parents and other family members in order to be saved for eternal life, is a profoundly interesting place from which to begin reflection about identity. It is an astonishing fact of our own pluralistic cultural situation of the present that structuralist and deconstructionist critiques have doubted the possibility of coherent identity for the individual, while researchers in another field, psychodynamic psychology, have been largely preoccupied during the last generation with clinical and theoretical studies of the self.

Object relations theory studies the permutations of the original, archaic relation of identity between mother and child throughout the life span of the human person. The quality of those first relationships determines to a great degree one's relationship to oneself, to others, and to the objects and institutions of the cultural environment in later phases of life, as the individual learns to differentiate her/himself from "other" ("das Andere," "whatever is not me"), and as *self objects* which once resided entirely in the person of the mother begin to assume correlative forms in the cultural objects and institutions with which the person interacts. There is by now very good experimental evidence to substantiate the work done in a clinical setting by analytic practitioners.[5]

Workers in clinical fields share a conviction which bridges theoretical differences on other points that individual identity, the self, emerges out of a delicately balanced series of developmental steps in which the individual at first identifies, and then gradually and partially dis-identifies, with the cultural matrix (the mother) while becoming more conscious of her/himself as a discrete person.[6] But the separation is always only partial. We continue throughout life to require recognition (we require to be "seen," as the mother first "sees" her child with acceptance and love in her eyes) and prestige from others in order to feel that we are anybody at all.[7]

2. Counter-cultural Phenomena and Religious Experience

What is of primary interest to me is not those cases in which the individual is successfully assimilated into the culture, but rather those cases in which the assimilation fails or is deliberately destroyed. Object relations theory addresses for the most part normative situations in which adaptation represents a successful outcome of development. It experiments in its clinical branches with healing through inducing therapeutic regression to the stage of the developmental failure, and then providing in the intimacy and trust of the therapy relationship a contained matrix for affective and cognitive re-learning. The goal of the process remains a relative cessation of psychic pain and reduction of anxiety, and the achieving of belonging participation in society.

Object relations theory is thus able to predict and to explain those cases in which the failure of positive social bonding produces excessive anxiety and psychic fragmentation. But it fails to provide a model to explain the successes which occur (that is, cases where fragmentation and overwhelming anxiety do not occur or are overcome) in spite of failures of bonding. Here we enter the realm of counter-cultural phenomena, and very frequently that of personal religious experience. My consideration of what it might have meant to leave the parents to seek salvation in the desert is focused upon this point.

Until fifty or so years ago, theological language seemed largely sufficient to describe and authenticate counter-cultural attitudes and experiences. This is no longer so. As a result of no longer having a fixed and ready conceptual container in which to fit these ideas and practices a debate has emerged whose surface level involves testing how the data fit within the knowledge field of various modern disciplines, but whose underlying theme has to do with crediting or discrediting religious experience and ascetic practice.

A good example of this process may be followed in the reaction to a late essay of Michel Foucault. Since he died before the fourth volume of his *History of Sexuality* series, *Confessions of the Flesh*, which was devoted to early Christian doctrine and experience, could be completed, his University of Vermont seminar, "Technologies of the Self," has been taken as a summary statement of his position (Foucault, 1988). Foucault claimed that the ascetic Christian practices of penitence and continual confession, accompanied as they were by a public, ritual character, and by the principle of absolute obedience to the master, had the effect of destroying the idea of a self which had been growing in Greco-Roman philosophical circles and had, outside Christianity, reached the level of actual practice. Christian renunciation is the villain of the story in Western history. Gedaliahu Stroumsa (1990) argued that Foucault was most certainly wrong. It was the emergence of a Christian doctrine of soul and body and the merging of Greek and Jewish traditions which resulted in the possibility of interiority which is first fully visible in Augustine. In the context of broad trends, wrote Stroumsa, more extreme ascetic practices should be seen as merely aberrant.

Patricia Cox Miller, in a 1989 paper read to the AAR, argued, rather, in favor of Foucault's idea. Christian contempt for the body, and for the desires and feelings emanating from the body, is written into the autobiographical text of the Christian fathers. It is then impossible for any new data entering into the field of consciousness (Cox Miller gives the example of a dream of Gregory of Nazianus showing his deceased brother in a glorious state) to modify the person's view of self in this world. Images of a beautiful body are pushed forward into the eschaton; body/self in the here and now remains mere dross.

I am in some sense convinced by each of these accounts. But I continue to be deeply moved by the suffering of the ascetic heroes, and by their great longing for the good. This connection of affectionate regard intimates some common ground of experience. We must try to find a way to believe in their story.

3. Cultural Instability of Opposing Ethical Precepts as Precursor of Fourth–Century Ascetic Movement

My general notion is that the fathers did not in fact renounce their parents, to live thenceforth without consolations. The parental image, and with it the efficacy of the parents in their role of providing security, sustenance and bonded relationships was moved from its initial location in the persons of the actual parents in the community where they lived, to another location inside the person of the ascetic pilgrim. In the language of object relations theory, the parental image was internalized. Insofar as this process of translocation was successful, and I mean of course, in this religious tradition, as goal of the practice, the ascetics' experience of God, they experienced relative autonomy and a relative freedom from overweening anxiety which finally enabled them to face death. Autonomy and freedom from excessive anxiety are the basic constituents of all current concepts of *self* which stem from clinical disciplines. What conditions in the culture and what techniques used by the ascetics might have enabled this result?

I offer the following considerations.

A. Stability/Instability in India and in Early Christian Culture

I propose that in the fourth century, and for various reasons having partly to do with the heritage of Alexandrian theology and with the geographical divisions of space in Egypt, the compromise solutions and the hierarchical formulas with which the Christian community had heretofore contained two diametrically opposed ethical precepts—the command to honor one's parents (by analogy and extension that includes the social community in which parental interests were invested) and the contradictory command to obey and follow Christ—broke down. The conflict could no longer be contained, and enmity broke out between opposing factions. One might characterize these opposed commandments along the lines proposed by Louis Dumont, who showed two strata in Indian society, one, an *inworldly* majority and the other an outworldly class of renouncers who comprised both mendicant wanderers and the monastic groups (Dumont, 1970). The only ethical requirement laid upon the inworldly laity was to support the *sangha*; this had already been pointed out by Max Weber. To the renouncer, however, belonged the task of carrying for the society its highest values; these values involved the development of the individual and disentanglement from human institutions, with a final goal of autonomy and then easy release from life. Dumont attempted to apply this Indian model to Western culture. Beginning with the Epicurean, Stoic and Cynic philosophies of the Hellenistic period, when Platonic and Aristotelian ideals of self-sufficiency were applied to the *individual* rather than to the *polis*, there developed a dichotomy between the wise man, who separates from the world, and the fool, who remains in it. This pattern seemed entirely similar to the situation in India. Christianity, according to Dumont—and here he follows the analysis of Ernst Troeltsch—reinforces the individualist ideals of the Hellenistic religions, "the individual soul [receiving] eternal value from its filial relationship to God."

The early Christians, says Dumont, were "nearer to the Indian renouncer than to ourselves," who have inherited that enormous cultural impetus (Dumont, 1986:25, 30, 32).

But the picture of an outworldly and an inworldly group which Dumont paints will not fit into the frame of Christian culture of the first centuries. It might well fit partially into an earlier Hellenistic period, when the wandering philosopher and the friends of Epicurus formed a real cultural elite. But the situation in India is that of an extremely stable, thousand–year–old milieu with well differentiated ethical expectations for each of the two religious classes. Ivan Strenski (465) has pointed out that it is actually a system of generalized exchange. The *sangha* has the duty of receiving gifts, and thus provides the principle opportunity for merit-making for lay people. The monks provide teaching, preaching, ritual performances; they enact for the culture an ideal life, but not in direct reciprocal exchange with those who provide for their bodily needs. Patterns of relationship are marked by qualitatively different ethical expectations for members of the two classes, but together they combine to describe the culture as a whole.

The difference between India and the culture of early Christianity is just this: Christianity collapsed social differences by placing the same ethical requirements on *all* its adherents. The new religion destabilized not only the larger culture; it also, and even more importantly for purposes of this discussion, created disorder and crisis among its members, at the level of parent-child relationships. This crisis could not be solved, but so long as the Roman Empire occupied the "inworldly" position, Christians might feel in general united as "outworldly," and formulaic solutions served just well enough. With the peace of Constantine that was no longer possible, for the Christians became now favored *in* the world. The trouble about identity stemming from contradictory commands, with their corollary contradictory ethical expectations of the Christian, boiled up in the middle of the Christian communities and split them apart.

B. *Bonded relations in families*

I have considered whether some other factor might explain more simply the extreme disavowal of parents in early and mid fourth–century Egypt. Perhaps low life expectancy for parents might have discouraged bonding. Many young people would have lost their parents before they themselves were fully grown. Among general causes for flight to the desert Robin Lane Fox has suggested changes in land ownership patterns, increased bureaucratization in local village life, and schisms and sects in the church as factors which drove Christians to the desert "in order to escape from their fellow Christians (603). "Inworldly" politics in the community are surely part and parcel of the politics of life inside the family.

Yet there is much evidence that family relationships could be very close and that Christian families were not different from pagan families except perhaps for their closer regard for each child as a gift of God; they very early rejected abortion and child exposure. Parents often had themselves painted together with their children. Gravemarkers give witness to children's tender love for parents; more than once a marker uses the childish word "tata" for father. Methodius mentions the joy of a mother who sees her children after a long separation. At the death of a son in whom one had great hopes Basil sends condolences to the mother as well as to the father.[8]

A common argument in favor of a daughter's taking the veil was that she as well as the members of her family might thereby avoid the sorrows which family life inevitably entails. In an early fourth-century homily a woman who chooses a husband will hold him in her arms only for a time, but weep and tear her hair and run up and down the streets barefooted in despair when his death is announced. "She will blame herself when her daughter dies and her son falls ill, when another misery threatens with her preceding misery, and groaning will follow after groaning" (Shaw: 34). Ambrose reminded parents how uncertain it was that their daughter's marriage would produce grandchildren; the path of virginity is a more certain road to advantage for the family (Ambrose, 1896:1.6.26, p.367). And John Chrysostom:

> First, it is not certain that a marriage will produce children at all; second, if children do come, there will be even greater discouragement. For the happiness which children bring us is far outweighed by the grief which comes from the daily care, anxiety, and fear which they cause (3.16, p.163).

Just how firm the bonds of affection in families could be is shown in Allison Elliott's recounting of early Christian legends. (Fiction or fact, the texts reveal psychological interpretations of experience which were then current.) Astion persuaded his mentor to sail away secretly with him to Scythia "lest my father pollute my unstained conscience with his tears." St. John Calybite feared his mother's tears, so pleaded with the monk with whom he would journey to Jerusalem that they should leave secretly. St. Benedict as a youth left his nurse without notice in order to go to the "desert" of Subiaco (Elliot: 87).

C. *Martyrdom as a cultural stabilizer and carrier of counter-cultural identity*

So long as the ideal of the perfect Christian as martyr lay within the purview of genuinely possible outcomes of faith, a Christian might carry on with life in the community, in or around the family, and at least not be totally cut off from familial relationships, without suffering undue anxiety at the level of personal identity as a soldier of Christ. One might be called to an ultimate destiny and still remain in pious obedience to the parents, after the same fashion as a man leaves father and mother to cleave to his wife.[10] Occasionally one even spoke of the Maccabean mother who led her seven sons to martyrdom (2 Macc 7:21-23; Ambrose, 1971:12.52-58, pp. 179-84).

But for all the prestige which might come to the martyr's family, for all the veneration received by the prospective martyr in prison, for all the grand feasts celebrated by the Church on the birthdays of the martyrs in heaven, there remained always the ineluctably *personal* experience of pain and death. This experience cannot be co-opted by any collective, politicized uses which are made of it. The potential of serving as martyr, because it involved a clearly envisionable content, or technique, namely suffering and death, anchored the Christian's sense of individual identity.

Robin Lane Fox has made a rather cynical analysis along the same lines, arguing that youthful innocence, an unreflective mind, and the fervor of the Church's insistence on faith as over against any possible more cautious consideration of the finality of death resulted in many wasted lives and very few conversions on the part of pagans. He writes very bluntly indeed:

> Behind every martyrdom . . . lay the self-sacrifice of Jesus himself. To be a Christian . . . was to recognize the supreme value of this selfless death at the hands of misguided authorities. At its heart, Christianity glorified suffering and passive endurance (441f.).

I sympathize with this assessment from the point of view of compassion for lives perhaps unnecessarily lost. (All wars should cause rage in the heart.) I believe however that the institution of martyrdom, because it served as a vehicle or container for individual identity, will have assumed an importance far in advance of its usefulness in increasing the numbers of converts.

I am working up to a hypothesis that identity as an individual, with its concomitant development of a "self," is a way of describing what we mean by counter-culture and counter-cultural identity. The antithetic pole is a culture of collective ideas which assimilates the individual. It is a very old idea that individuality for any but a philosophical elite emerged in the West together with the Christian religion (Troeltsch: 1.52-58). This idea is still useful, if we can be more precise in describing how that may have been possible.

The ideal object which was first located in the persons of the parents is transferred to an internalized ideal object which represents the highest value. The values attendant on this ideal are the high values in the culture, but they can be obtained by the individual only with the greatest difficulty. There is a technique or a practice which leads to the goal. Neither the *values* nor the *technique* are mere intellectual counters; they reproduce in their fullness of passion and commitment the emotional climate of the primal relationship between parent and child in which object cathexis is first achieved. Over the trajectory of affect a transition from parent to internalized self object can be made.

The martyr who believed he/she would go directly to Christ has completed a process of internalizing the self object which is completely valid because it has as its primary symbolic content caring parental love.[11] This parental love is rooted in the biological conditions for survival of an order in which development in the womb is approximately a year shorter than the complexity of the species relative to other mammals would require, and in which maturation to independence requires many years of nurturance in a social matrix (Portmann: 355f.). It does not matter whether there were just a few instances of a high level of integration of Christ within, and many imitations; what matters is that the way was known.

With the collapse of martyrdom as a carrier of the *technique* of achieving individual identity (or salvation), the precarious balance between opposing commandments to honor one's parents and to follow and obey Christ also collapsed. There was no longer a clear image in the Christian community of how the high value—that which differentiated the Christian from the non-Christian—was to be achieved. Though the term has been overused in popular culture of recent years it would be correct to name the situation an identity crisis. What the crisis is about is painful conflict and the danger of regression to a more primitive level of development if the conflict cannot be solved. In the fourth century there were not yet two classes of Christians, one with a lesser ethical mandate and one with the fuller commandment to perfection. The full commandment lay upon all Christians. It is in this light that I believe the urgency of fourth-century quests for salvation may be better understood.

4. Ascetic Technique and Stoic Vocabulary

The pattern of relationship between technique used (passion and suffering) and goal achieved (union with Christ) during the period of martyrdom was very similar to the technique used to reach that same goal by the ascetics who followed the martyrs, but the Stoic vocabulary of the ascetic texts may have obscured this similarity. We must again refer to the Antonian *Vita*, not only because it is historically a model text, but because the dramatic composition of the text allows us to study the ascetics' lives as they ought to have happened, in the mind of Athanasius and his contemporaries.

During the first stage of his disciplinary preparation, while living in the tombs beyond his village, Anthony felt over and over again that he was completely beaten up by the devil, enough that he might die of the pain. Finally the roof opened, a beam of light descended, and Anthony felt the presence of God. Anthony was relieved of his pains but reproached God for having left him so alone and for having allowed him to suffer. Then the voice of God came to him: "I was here, Antony, but I waited to watch your struggle. And now, since you persevered and were not defeated, I will be your helper forever" (Athanasius, 1980: chap. 10, p. 39). The parents whose memory Anthony left behind with his first decision for the ascetic path have now been internalized as a parenting God, as a result of Anthony's lonely struggle with himself, and of impositions on the body which result in pain.

During the second stage of his discipline, hidden in the fortress of the outer mountain, Anthony was again persecuted by devils, whose noise sounded like mobs of interlopers to the friends who occasionally passed bread down to him from above. But Anthony now felt support against the demons through his beneficent visions. He no longer felt physically injured by bad spirits. He counseled his friends that they could fortify themselves with the sign of the cross and leave with confidence. When at last he was forced to come forth and show himself, because so many would-be ascetics sought his teaching, his body seemed perfect and unchanged by the rigors of his ascesis:

> The state of his soul was pure, for it was neither contracted by grief, nor dissipated by pleasure nor pervaded by jollity or dejection. He was not embarrassed when he saw the crowd, nor was he elated at seeing so many others there to receive him. No, he had himself completely under control—a man guided by reason and stable in his character (Athanasius, 1978: chap. 14, p. 32).

On the surface, this passage presents a Stoic image of the wise man who has reached the stage of *apatheia*. But the monistic Stoic universe is incoherent in the world of Anthony and his fellow ascetics. No personal God watches over the Stoic's efforts to obtain equanimity; practicants were on their own in this respect. The Stoic technique of dealing with suffering, at least with those matters not under one's own control, is a kind of cognitive reprogramming which admits that suffering is a meaningless act of false judgment and which determines therefore not to keep the memory of sorrow and pain "green" by continually calling it to mind (Cicero: 3.30.74; 31.75, p. 314f.).[12] I take it that the desert ascetics practiced just the opposite technique. By their continual punishment of their bodies they kept their suffering green.

The Christianized Stoicism of Clement of Alexandria comes closer in language to the Antonian text, and here at least we may refer to a historically direct line of influence on Athanasius' composition. Clement's true gnostic "shares in the affections of the body ... yet is not primarily affected by passion. In the accidents which befall him against his will, he raises himself from his troubles ... and is not carried away by things which have nothing to do with true self" (Clement, 1954:7.62, p. 132). Clement is an ascetic, but a gentler spirit than the desert fathers who followed him in Egypt. The soul for Clement is indeed above the body, but "all things are of one God."

> Those who run down created existence and vilify the body are wrong. . . . The constitution of man . . . which has its place among things of sense, was necessarily composed of things diverse, but not opposite—body and soul. . . . Now the soul of the wise man and Gnostic, as sojourning in the body, conducts itself towards it gravely and respectfully, not with inordinate affections, as about to leave the tabernacle if the time of departure summons (Clement, 1885:4.26, p. 439f.).

It seems to me that the fourth-century ascetic fathers were engaged in a more violent kind of game. In Mark Helprin's marvelous new novel, *A Soldier of the Great War*, the hero Alessandro explains to his still callow young friend Nicolò why he always sleeps on the floor. "Because the floor is hard and cold," said Alessandro. "I don't believe this," said Nicolò.

> "I'm not asking you to be a nun," Alessandro told him. "I'm not asking you to do anything. I'm just telling you that the intellect is of no use unless it's disciplined by the mortification of the flesh, so that it may serve the soul. That's all. The intellect thinks. The body dances. And the spirit sings. A song, a simple song. When love and memory are overwhelming, and the soul, though crushed, takes flight, it does so in a simple song."
> "How do you know this?"
> "I've heard it."
> "What does it say?"
> "It says, at the very end, in the last distillation of all you know, that you have only one thing left, one thing that might travel, though God only knows how" (729).

Like Alessandro, who sleeps on the floor in order to cause a song within to form, the desert fathers with their ascetic practices kept themselves in a nearly constant state of emotional arousal so that their salvation (their inner self, in modern terms) could form itself within. Ascetics prayed constantly. They fought with devils in the air. They were always at the business of analyzing their own motives. They advised unflagging zeal as the path to the goal. By limiting contact with the outer world they were able to focus their entire attention on internal states. When accompanied by certain standards as a safe limiting frame, namely the religious ideals of the culture, this being bathed in affect may have served the same function that the mother's seeing and holding of the child in her arms serves in more natural circumstances, and thus be an alternate path to the self. The self so formed may properly be named a countercultural identity.

This theoretical reformulation is consistent with object relations theories of human development, while going a step beyond to explain how failures of adaptation may nevertheless result in strong individuals and in creative achievements. There are many ways in which one may lose the benefits of one's parents and several possible outcomes of such losses. In moments of its history, the values carried by the Christian religion have offered the possibility for non-repressive acceptance of the suffering which is part of all life, and have at the same time shown a way to create moral values out of weakness and loss.

In our eyes, looking back into a culture not our own, the artificial induction of suffering practiced by the ascetics is ethically and psychologically most questionable. But it did not seem so in the fourth century. With the demise of the institution of martyrdom it became necessary to redefine in terms of action and technique what it meant to be a Christian. A radical differentiation between the Christian individual and society was needed. It was for this reason that exemplary ascetics—Anthony, Pachomius, Theodore, Ammon—left parents and homes completely.

The vocabulary of *apatheia* belongs then not to the *technique* of achieving a self—it could never belong there and make any kind of sense at all for the same human being that modern social science knows anything about—but rather to the self which is achieved as a result of practice. This is the self which Athanasius describes as pure in soul, neither depressed nor inflated, nor overly vulnerable to the influence of the crowd, but a person "stable in character," guided by reason and in control of himself. The language describing the Stoic wise man is still not quite right, but it is the best conceptual language available in the fourth century.[13] It also meets the criteria which I have set out above for a basic, non-metaphysical definition of the self, as a condition of relative autonomy and relative freedom from excessive anxiety.

5. The Ascetic Hero and Social Change.

The achievement of individual autonomy is however always only for a moment. As soon as "an individual behavior" becomes widely accepted it is politicized, institutionalized and taken over by the power structures of the society. By the end of the fourth century Ambrose was advising parents that a virgin in the family helps with her services to save the parents from their sins (Ambrose, 1896:1.7.32, p.368).[14] Chrysostom titillates the possessive pride of parents even while he exhorts them to give their children to the monastic life. Parents may choose whether their sons shall hold rank "in the front row, gazing with confidence upon the archangels, or stuck back in the crowd, in the very last place." The spiritual children of their children's union with God will be more glorious than any real grandchildren could be. Much more satisfactory than gaining such power that one can take revenge on those who have harmed you, is becoming so invulnerable that no one at all can harm you. Thus parents should prefer the monastic vocation for their sons (3.18, p. 166; 16, p. 162; 2.6, p. 110). In the desert, the authority and influence of the bishops soon mitigated the initial strictness of separations between parents and their children who became monks, abbots finding it politic to take a more flexible stand.[15]

If there is any relationship between the presently available, probably eleventh–century text and the early fourth– to fifth–century original Greek version of the *Canons of Athanasius* (and Riedel thought there was), it was not long before every Christian family was required to have at least one virgin. She served an apotropaic function in warding off the wrath which might come upon a whole city (97). If a family should choose a daughter to serve as virgin and she is disobedient and does not wish to serve, she should be kept at home until she is thirty years old and then appointed. She may be struck and reproached, so that she realizes the solemnity of promises made on her behalf (98). In the processions from the monastery to the church the nuns should go two by two holding hands. If any nun should let her hand fall from the sister nun who is holding it she shall be punished, "because she erred in the midst of her people" (92).

Here we have fine, if very sad, illustrations of the way in which achievements marking autonomous development are co-opted into the social institutions of society. Louis Dumont's hierarchical theory of cultural change seems to suit the facts well. New ideas stemming from the outworldly element of society, once they are successfully received, undergo modifications as they are assimilated into the inworldly culture, breaking down the differences between once heterogenous elements and uniting the field under the aegis of the once outworldly high value (Dumont, 1986: 17f., 32).[16] Thus Christianity, originating as a powerful counter-cultural fragment of Western culture, became over the course of several centuries the guarantor of a stable social order. The culturally destabilizing split between inworldly and outworldly values, exhibited in early Christian culture by irreconcilable ethical demands to honor parents and to follow Christ, was healed in later centuries as the Church developed two classes of Christians, and two levels of perfection.

For the individual, the institutional assimilation of individual values means a continual need to reassess the current situation in order to discover a moral stance, and a path of action and thought.[17]

NOTES

[1] The condition of being "homeless" (*anagārika*) also characterizes the renouncer's life throughout traditional Buddhism, cutting across variations between groups which differ on other points (Carrithers: 41ff.).

[2] Goehring believes that the Bohairic Life is earliest, and places it in the mid-fourth century. He reasons that the later growth of the movement necessarily entailed greater involvement of ecclesiastical authorities from the towns and a consequent increased pressure from parental interests with a softening of the earlier strict stance of monks and abbots on relationship with parents (Goehring, 1986:117, 178f., 266f., 279f.; 1990:350f.). For a summary of disputes concerning primacy among various Pachomian Lives see Chadwick (1981:15ff.). If the Bohairic text is indeed early, then it represents the first sharp impetus of the great movement to the desert.

[3] See also the Draguet Fragment (Veilleux: 2:115). Other references to relationship between the monk and family are in Ruppert. "Pachomius hält es für ideal, das Gebot des Evangeliums so zu verwirklichen, dass man jeden Kontakt mit den Angehörigen meidet. Er selbst hat sich auch so verhalten, als seine Schwester ihn besuchen wollte. Trotzdem fordert er von den anderen nicht dieselbe Haltung" (142–51).

[4] Matt 8:21–2; 12:48–50; 19:29; Mark 1:20; 3:31–35 and parallels; 10:30; Luke 2:48–50; 9:57–62 and parallels; 14:26 and parallels; 1 Cor 4:15.

[5] The pioneering work of John Bowlby in the 1950s and 1960s may be mentioned. Ethological studies on social bonding in the work of Konrad Lorenz, Niko Tinbergen and Irenaeus Eibl-Eibesfeldt demonstrate a phylogenetically pre-programmed basis in the organism for attachment.

[6] Greenberg and Mitchell give detailed summaries of leading theorist/practitioners. Kohut and Wolf present a clinical summary of terms in their Self Psychology. Winnicott has a useful introduction by M. Masud R. Khan.

[7] Taylor makes this point neatly (36–38). The "defining community" comprises our language group as well as those with whom we feel closer affinity. Both are necessary in order for us to achieve self-definition.

[8] RAC 4:1209, 1217–18. Basil's letter to Nestorius reads: "I need not say how grieved I was nor how many tears I shed.... The heir of an illustrious house... the hope of his father... in the very flower of his youth has been snatched from the hands of his parents and is gone from our midst." To Nestorius' wife Basil writes: "I know how deep are the affections of mothers.... You have lost a son whom, while he lived, all mothers blessed and prayed that their own sons might resemble" (Letters 5 and 6).

[9] I am grateful to James Goehring for mentioning this book to me. For other references see Browning: 120f.

[10] RAC 4:1214. For third–century anticipations of the greater splits which would develop in the fourth century see Chadwick (1981).

[11] Ignatius of Antioch writes of "reaching God" by following in the footsteps of Paul, who died a martyr. He begs the Romans not to hinder his martyrdom, for he will never have a better opportunity of reaching God. To Polycarp he writes that he is comforted and without a care in God, or will be, if only through suffering he can reach God (*Eph.* 12; *Rom.* 2; *Polycarp* 7). Perpetua and Saturus envision their arrival after

death in a garden where an aged, white-haired man greets them with milk, a paternal kiss, and an instruction that they could "go and play" (4.25, 12.20 in Musurillo).

[12] "So long as the imagined evil preserves a certain power of being vigorous and retaining so to speak its greeness, it is termed 'fresh.'" See Kaelber, esp. chap. 4, for a description of a process which seems more similar to the technique of Christian ascetics than to the Stoic program.

[13] For another view of the relationship between Stoic vocabulary and the Christian theology of the desert see Gregg and Groh. Chap. 4, and esp. p. 146, refers to the text under present discussion. Gregg sees God's voice, "I was here, Antony," as an expression of Athanasius' anti-Arian doctrine of grace. Gregg and Groh's general thesis, that the Arian disputes had as their root theme soteriological issues, is consonant with ideas expressed here. The trustworthiness of Athanasius' hagiographical biography of Anthony has always been somewhat clouded by questions concerning Athanasius' personal character. At least one recent study concludes that "the bishop deserves a better fate than to serve future generations continually as an example of a fourth-century gangster or an unscrupulous church politician" (Wade-Hampton: 186).

[14] This, and the examples which follow, might be seen as defining in their terms of exchange the contents of the culture in which this sort of exchange existed. See Strenski. The person whose achievement of individual identity is co-opted by the culture experiences either a power inflation or betrayal of self by the inworldly group. A third alternative, which might not exclude either of the first two alternatives, is to become a cultural hero. See Hook.

[15] See n. 2 above.

[16] Kaelber discusses Dumont's "challenge and assimilation" model versus J. C. Heesterman's "orthogenetic" model for understanding the emergence of and the tension between the individual and society in Brahmanic India (105–109).

[17] C. G. Jung was the first social scientist to ground an entire theory in the search for individual values.

WORKS CONSULTED

Ambrose of Milan
    1896   "*Concerning Virgins.*" Pp. 363–387 in *St. Ambrose: Select Works and Letters*. Trans. E. De Romestin. NPNF Second Series 10. New York: The Christian Literature Company.

    1971   "Jacob and the Happy Life." Pp. 117–184 in *Saint Ambrose: Seven Exegetical Works*. Trans. Michael P. McHugh. FC 65. Washington: Catholic University of America Press.

Athanasius
    1978   *The Life of St. Antony.* Trans. Robert T. Meyer. ACW 10. New York: Newman.

    1980   *The Life of Antony and the Letter to Marcellinus.* Ed. and Trans. Robert C. Gregg. Classics of Western Spirituality. New York: Paulist.

Basil of Caesarea
 1951   *Letters*. Vol. 1 (1–185) Trans. Sr. Agnes Clare Way. FC 13. Washington: Catholic University of America Press.

Bowlby, John
 1969,   *Attachment and Loss*. 2 vols. London: Hogarth.
 1973

Browning, Robert
 1981   "The 'Low Level' Saint's Life in the Early Byzantine World." Pp. 117–127 in *The Byzantine Saint: University of Birmingham Fourteenth Spring Symposium of Byzantine Studies*. Ed. Sergei Hackel. Sobornost.

Carrithers, Michael
 1983   *The Forest Monks of Sri Lanka: An Anthropological and Historical Study*. Delhi: Oxford University Press.

Cassian, John
 1978   *The Conferences*. Trans. Edgar C. S. Gibson. Pp. 291–546 in
 rpt.   *Sulpitius Severus. Vincent of Lerins. John Cassian*. NPNF Second Series 11. Grand Rapids: Eerdmanns.

Chadwick, Henry
 1981   "Pachomios and the Idea of Sanctity." Pp. 11–24 in *The Byzantine Saint: University of Birmingham Fourteenth Spring Symposium of Byzantine Studies*. Ed. Sergei Hackel. Sobornost.

Cicero
 1971   *Cicero in Twenty Eight Volumes*. Vol. 18. *Tusculan Disputations*. Trans. J. E. King. LCL 141. Cambridge: Harvard University Press.

Clement of Alexandria
 1885   "The Miscellanies." Pp. 299–568 in *Fathers of the Second Century*. Trans. W. Wilson. ANF 2. Buffalo: The Christian Literature Company.
 1954   "On Marriage" (*Miscellanies* 3) and "On Spiritual Perfection" (*Miscellanies* 7). Pp. 15–165 in *Alexandrian Christianity*. Trans. Henry Chadwick. LCC. Philadelphia: Westminster.

Dumont, Louis
 1970   "World Renunciation in Indian Religions." Pp. 33–61 in *Religion, Politics and History in India*. Ed. Louis Dumont. Paris: Mouton.

1986 "Genesis, I," Pp. 23–60 in *Essays on Individualism: Modern Ideology in Anthropological Perspective*. Chicago: University of Chicago Press.

Elliott, Alison Goddard
1987 *Roads to Paradise: Reading the Lives of the Early Saints*. Hanover and London: Brown University Press.

Foucault, Michel
1988 "Technologies of the Self." Pp. 16–49 in *Technologies of the Self: A Seminar with Michel Foucault*, Ed. Luther H. Martin, Huck Gutman, and Patrick H. Hutton. Amherst: University of Massachusetts Press.

Fox, Robin Lane
1988 *Pagans and Christians*. San Francisco: Harper & Row.

Goehring, James
1986 *The Letter of Ammon and Pachomian Monasticism*. Patristische Texte und Studien 27. Berlin: Walter de Gruyter.
1990 "Theodore's Entry into the Pachomian Movement," Pp. 349–356 in *Ascetic Behavior in Greco-Roman Antiquity*. Ed. Vincent L. Wimbush, Studies in Antiquity and Christianity. Minneapolis: Fortress.

Greenberg, Jay R., and Stephen A. Mitchell
1983 *Object Relations in Psychoanalytic Theory*. Cambridge: Harvard University Press.

Gregg, Robert C., and Dennis E. Groh
1980 *Early Arianism—A View of Salvation*. Philadelphia: Fortress.

Gregory of Nyssa
1967 "The Life of Saint Macrina." Pp. 161–97 in *Saint Gregory of Nyssa: Ascetical Works*. Trans. Virginia Woods Callahan. FC 58. Washington: Catholic University of America Press.

Helprin, Mark
1991 *A Soldier of the Great War*. New York: Harcourt Brace Jovanovich.

Hook, Sidney
1955 *The Hero in History: A Study in Limitation and Possibility*. Boston: Beacon.

Ignatius of Antioch
    1947   "St. Ignatius of Antioch: The Letters." Pp. 83–127 in *The Apostolic Fathers*. Trans. Gerald G. Walsh. FC 1. Washington: Catholic University of America Press.

John Chrysostom
    1988   *A Comparison Between a King and a Monk/Against the Opponents of the Monastic Life*. Ed. and Trans. David G. Hunter. Studies in the Bible and Early Christianity 13. Lewiston: Edwin Mellen.

Jung, C. G.
    1964   "The Undiscovered Self." Pp. 245–262 in *Collected Works* 10. Bollingen Series 20. New York: Pantheon.

Kaelber, Walter O.
    1989   *Tapta Mārga: Asceticism and Initiation in Vedic India*. Albany: SUNY Press.

Kohut, Heinz, and Ernest S. Wolf
    1978   "The Disorders of the Self and their Treatment: An Outline." *International Journal of Psychoanalysis* 59:413–25.

Miller, Patricia Cox
    1989   "Dreams and (Auto)biography in Early Christian Writing." Paper presented at the annual meeting of the American Academy of Religion, Anaheim, California. Now published as "Re-Imagining the Self in Dreams." *Continuum* 1:35–53.

Musurillo, Herbert, ed. and trans.
    1972   "The Martyrdom of Saints Perpetua and Felicitas." Pp. 106–131 in *The Acts of the Christian Martyrs*. Oxford: Clarendon.

Origen
    1954   "*Exhortation to Martyrdom*." Pp. 388–429 in *Alexandrian Christianity*. Trans. Henry Chadwick. LCC. Philadelphia: Westminster.

Portmann, Adolf
    1954   "Biology and the Phenomenon of the Spiritual." Pp. 342–370 in *Spirit and Nature*. Vol. 1 of *Papers from the Eranos Yearbooks*. Bollingen Series 30. New York: Pantheon.

Riedel, Wilhelm, and W. E. Crum, eds. and trans.
    1904   *The Canons of Athanasius of Alexandria: The Arabic and Coptic Versions*. London: Williams and Norgate.

Ruppert, Fidelis
1971 *Das Pachomianische Mönchtum und die Anfänge Klösterlichen Gehorsams.* Münsterschwarzach: Vier Türme Verlag.

Shaw, Teresa M.
1990 "Homily: *On Virginity.*" Pp. 29–44 in *Ascetic Behavior in Greco-Roman Antiquity.* Ed. Vincent L. Wimbush. Studies in Antiquity and Christianity. Minneapolis: Fortress.

Strenski, Ivan
1983 "On Generalized Exchange and the Domestication of the Sangha." *MAN* n.s. 18:463–77.

Stroumsa, Gedaliahu G.
1990 "*Caro salutis cardo:* Shaping the Person in Early Christian Thought." HR 30:25–50.

Taylor, Charles
1989 *Sources of the Self: The Making of the Modern Identity.* Cambridge: Harvard University Press.

Troeltsch, Ernst
1949 *The Social Teaching of the Christian Churches.* 2 vol. Trans. Olive Wyon. Glencoe, IL: The Free Press.

Veilleux, Armand, trans.
1980– *Pachomian Koinonia: The Lives, Rules, and Other Writings*
1982 *of Saint Pachomius and his Disciples.* 3 vols. Cistercian Studies Series 45. Kalamazoo, MI: Cistercian.

Wade-Hampton, Duane
1991 *The Early Episcopal Career of Athanasius of Alexandria.* Notre Dame: University of Notre Dame Press.

Winnicott, D. W.
1975 *Through Paediatrics to Psycho-Analysis.* New York: Basic Books.

THROUGH A GLASS DARKLY: DIVERSE IMAGES OF THE *APOTAKTIKOI(AI)* OF EARLY EGYPTIAN MONASTICISM[1]

James E. Goehring
Mary Washington College

ABSTRACT

Increasing papyrological evidence of the use of the term *apotaktikos* as a label for certain Egyptian ascetics raises the question of the term's definition vis-à-vis the more traditional categories of the anchoritic and coenobitic monk. A simple solution is not possible, because the term *apotaktikos* on occasion overlaps the traditional divisions. In this paper, I will argue that the problem lies not in the Egyptian use of the term *apotaktikos*, but in the attempt to interpret it in terms of an understanding of Egyptian monasticism based on literary models. When one begins with the Egyptian evidence for the *apotaktikoi* and not with the literary definitions of anchorite and coenobite derived from Jerome and Cassian, the Egyptian use of the term *apotaktikos* becomes clearer and the picture of Egyptian monasticism more complex.

Introduction

Increasing numbers of documentary papyri relevant to the study of early Egyptian monasticism have, in recent years, inaugurated new discussions on the precise meaning of the "technical" term *apotaktikos* and its relationship to the more common "technical" terms *anachōrētēs* and *koinobiōtēs*.[2] While basic agreement can be found among scholars, the diverse theories put forward to explain the various usages of the term *apotaktikos* underscore the complexity of the problem. I intend to argue here that the problem lies not in the Egyptian use of the term, but rather in the influence of non-Egyptian literary models of Egyptian monasticism on our understanding of the Egyptian movement. The impact of the literary ideals of the *anachōrētēs*, understood as the solitary hermit epitomized by Anthony, and the *koinobiōtēs*, viewed as a fully communal monk of the Pachomian type, has created a simplified bi-polar understanding of Egyptian monasticism in which the term *apotaktikos* does not fit. In the pages that follow, a careful analysis of the evidence of the *apotaktikoi* in Egypt will be used to challenge this bi-polar view of Egyptian monasticism and argue that the historical reality is better served by the notion of a complex continuum from the fully solitary monk to the fully communal monk. As will be shown, the diversity in the use of the term *apotaktikos* derives precisely from the existence of such a continuum.

Apotaktikos, Anachoretes, and Koinobiotes: A Question of Community

The scholarly debate over the meaning of *apotaktikos* illustrates the difficulty presented by the varied use of the term in diverse literary and documentary sources. A. Lambert, writing in 1907 before the publication of the documentary evidence, held that a clear distinction must be maintained between the use of the term *apotaktikoi* in Egypt and its parallel form, *apotaktikai*, in the areas of Asia Minor and Palestine. While the latter term served to label a particular class of Christians who chose an austere life marked by the abandonment of worldly goods, the wearing of clothing (a costume) indicative of poverty and a practice of rigorous fasting and self-denial, the use of the parallel *apotaktikoi* in Egypt, where the notion of withdrawal (*anachōrēsis*) predominated, was purely adjectival. It served, according to Lambert, as but one among many qualifiers defining the monastic life.

Seventy years later, E. A. Judge, on the basis of more recently published documentary evidence, set the distinction between Egypt and the more northern provinces aside. He saw in the references to *apotaktikoi* in the papyri evidence of an early apotactic movement that originated in an urban setting and preceded the subsequent anchoritic and coenobitic developments in Egyptian monasticism (Judge, 1977:72–89; cf. 1981:613–20). In Judge's view, the *apotaktikoi* came to represent a class of ascetics in Egypt, men who "at last followed the pattern long set for virgins and widows, and set up houses of their own in town, in which the life of personal renunciation and service in the church would be practiced" (1977:85). According to Judge, the subsequent development of anchoritic monasticism, epitomized by Antony's withdrawal from the civic community, and coenobitic monasticism, associated with Pachomius's separate walled ascetic "villages" (Brown, 1988:245–46), rapidly overshadowed the apotactic movement in the middle to latter half of the fourth century. In turn, the literary efforts of such churchmen as Athanasius (*Vita Antonii*) and Jerome (*Ep*. 22) to capture the monastic movement for their ecclesio-political camp, in part by identifying its "pure" or "true" form with these later anchoritic and coenobitic developments,[3] resulted in the relegation of the apotactic movement to the fringes of the emerging literary history of Egyptian monasticism and the linkage of its later practitioners in that history to the shadowy world of charlatans and heretics.[4]

The shift in the scholarly interpretation of the term *apotaktikos* in Egyptian sources could hardly be more acute. The documentary evidence, often legal in nature, suggested a more technical meaning of the term; it was more than an adjective. Its use alone seemed to define an individual as a particular type of ascetic, a use that paralleled that of the term *apotaktikai* in the northern provinces. Acceptance of this conclusion, however, still left undefined the precise nature of ascesis practiced by the *apotaktikoi*.

The place of the *apotaktikoi* in relationship to the "more traditional" categories of *anachōrētai* and *koinobiōtai* depends on both the particular source or sources one is considering and the nature of the renunciation (*apotaxis*) one associates with the name. Judge's definition, which distinguishes the *apotaktikoi* from the other two categories, has its origin not in the documentary papyri, but in the connection he draws between Jerome's third class of Egyptian ascetics, the *remnuoth*, who lived in small household groups within the cities, and Julian's *apotaktikai*, a sub-group of Christians to whom Julian likens the Cynics in an attempt to disparage them (Jerome, *Ep.* 22.34; Julian, *Or.* 7.18; Judge, 1977:78–80). With respect to these inner-city ascetics or *apotaktikoi*, the papyri serve in Judge's analysis simply to add additional elements to a basic definition already derived from these non-Egyptian literary sources (1977:80–83; cf. 1981:613–20). From the papyri, one learns that *apotaktikos* was a church rank (P. Wurzb. 16), that the *apotaktikos* could own land (P. Flor. 71, 722), that he might retain family ties (P. Lips. 28), that the title later came to include women (P. Oxy. XLIV 3203), and that it served to indicate an ascetic's more active position within the civil community in distinction from the less active role of the *anachōrētēs* (P. Herm. 9).

Judge's use of Jerome's three-fold division of Egyptian monasticism (*coenobium*,[5] *anachoretae*, and *remnuoth* in *Ep.* 22.34–35; cf. Cassian's *coenobiotae*, *anachoretae* and *sarabaitae* in his *Conf.* 18.4), suggests a distinction of the *apotaktikos*, at least originally, from the later *anachōrētēs* and *koinobiōtēs*.[6] When one turns to the papyri and Egyptian literary sources alone, however, the situation is less clear. The editor of P. Oxy. 3203, a lease agreement dated to 400 CE in which the lessors are two sisters titled *monachoi apotaktikai*, linked the label *apotaktikos* more closely to the anchoritic form of monasticism, since the anchoritic monk, as opposed to the coenobitic monk, could own property (Haslam: 183). This conclusion is based on the observation that *apotaktikai*, according to the papyrus in question, could own property and on the assumption, drawn from the Pachomian model, that coenobitic monks could not own property.[7]

The link between the terms *apotaktikos* and *anachōrētēs* is further supported in the four letters that form the archive of Apa Johannes (P. Herm. 7–10). In this collection, Apa Johannes is twice called *anachōrētēs* and once *apotaktikos*. While the texts do not offer any specific clarification of the use of the two terms, it seems fair to conclude that in some manner at least they must overlap.[8] If Judge is correct in equating the *apotaktikoi* with

Jerome's *remnuoth*, then in the figure of Apa Johannes, we have an ascetic who somehow straddles two of Jerome's three categories.[9]

While the above documents suggest a link between the terms *apotaktikos* and *anachōrētēs*, other texts seem to equate *apotaktikos* with *koinobiōtēs*. A list of tax payments made in the Hermopolite nome in 367–368 CE (P. Berl. inv. 11860 A-B; Wipszycka) includes a payment made by the *apotaktikos* Anoubion for land belonging to the monastery of Tabennese. Since Tabennese was the first community established by Pachomius, whose *koinōnia* serves generally to define coenobitic monasticism, the term *apotaktikos* in this text appears to serve as a virtual synonym for *koinobiōtēs*. It is possible, though far from certain, that other documents that record land ownership by an *apotaktikos* (P. Herm. Landl.) or the payment of land tax (CPR V 26) by a *monache*, whose monastic affiliation is not specified, should be understood in this context. In other words, the monk did not own the land himself, but simply paid the taxes for land owned by his monastic community (Judge, 1981:618; Krause, 1985:123).

At any rate, it is clear from the literary sources that the Pachomian community used the term *apotaktikos* as a self-designation for its members. The Coptic recensions of the *Vita Pachomii* employ the term *apotaktikos* (ⲢⲰⲘⲈ ⲚⲀⲠⲞⲦⲀⲔⲦⲒⲔⲞⲤ) as a label for Pachomian monks (Lefort, 1925:233 s.v.; 1933:379 s.v.; Krause, 1985:122–23), and the Greek *Excerpta* of the Pachomian *Regula* specifically refers to new members as those who "come to the monastery to become an *apotaktikos*" (*ean tis proselthē tē monē elthōn genesthai apotaktikos*; Recension B, sec. 49; Boon: 174; Krause, 1985:122; Wipszycka: 633). In addition, two Coptic sources, a catechesis attributed to Pachomius (Lefort, 1956:16.32–34 [text], 17.23–25 [translation]) and a letter attributed to Athanasius (Lantshoot: 274 [text], 287 [translation]), incorporate *apotaktikos* into a threefold division of Egyptian monasticism. In place of Jerome's three categories of *coenobium*, *anachoretae* and *remnuoth*, one finds in these Coptic sources *parthenoi*, *apotaktikoi*, and *anachōrētai*. The *parthenoi* likely refer to female ascetics, and the *anachōrētai* are the solitary hermits. The *apotaktikoi*, as a result, must, in this Coptic tradition, refer to those ascetics who, in modern scholarly circles, on the basis of Jerome's and Cassian's respective use of *coenobium* and *coenobiotae*, are more commonly termed coenobites.

The blurring of the terminology of *apotaktikos* and *koinobiōtēs* is further suggested by the early fifth century diary of Egeria. She distinguishes three types of monks found in the east: *ascites*, *monazontes*, and *apotaktikai*. However, while the *ascites* remain distinct throughout the diary, the *monazontes* and *apotaktikai* seem at points to blend into one another (Maraval: 229 n. 3; cf. Judge, 1977: 80). It seems likely that the *ascites* represent the *anachōrētai* and the *monazontes* some form of the *koinobiōtai*. While the difficulties in understanding the distinction between the *apotaktikai* and the *monazontes* in the diary could be explained by a weak talent for details on Egeria's part, it seems most likely in view of the other evidence cited above that the overlap in the use of the two terms simply reflects the current situation in Egeria's day.

It thus appears from the evidence that the term *apotaktikos*, at least by the middle of the fourth century (P. Berl. inv. 11860), was current in Egypt as a title for ascetic individuals who chose to practice their ascesis within a community of like-minded persons (Wipszycka: 634).[10] That it came to be used by the Pachomian monks, who clearly distinguished themselves from the *anachoretae* (Bohairic *Vita Pachomii* [*Bo*] 134 = Greek *Vita prima* [*G1*] 136; cf. *Bo* 67 = *G1* 72), as a self-designation suggests that the community element was inherent in the term from an early point in its history.

Alanna Emmett has suggested that the occurrence of the combined form of *monachai apotaktikai* in P. Oxy. 3203 argues for the use of *apotaktikos* as a word of specification designed to distinguish a particular type of monk (511–12). I would suggest that it distinguishes a monk who lives communally from one who chose to practice a more solitary ascesis. The latter form of ascesis is most associated with the term *anachōrētēs*, a connection fostered especially by Athanasius' *Vita Antonii*. The hardening of the term *anachōrētēs* as a technical term for a monk who withdrew to a solitary life led likewise to the need, on occasion, to qualify that term. Such qualification was necessary since a solitary lifestyle did not necessarily imply total isolation or lack of some form of community. A letter from the mid-fourth century (P. Lond VI 1925; Bell, 1924:106–8), for example, is addressed to an *anachōrētēs monēs monachon* so as to indicate that the monk in question led an anchoritic lifestyle within a community of monks (Emmett: 511–12).[11] In the Pachomian sources, which clearly distinguish their communal practice from the anchoritic lifestyle, Theodore, before he joined the Pachomian community, is likewise said to have entered "a monastery in the nome of Sne where he led an anchoritic life with some old and pious monks" (*Bo* 31; cf. Goehring, 1990a). In all likelihood, it is just such a situation that accounts for the use of both *anachōrētēs* and *apotaktikos* as titles for Apa Johannes in P. Herm 7–10 (supra pp. 5–6). Apa Johannes lived in a community of solitary monks. His solitary nature allows for the title *anachōrētēs*, and his existence in a community of such monks for the title *apotaktikos*.

It is thus clear that while the term *apotaktikos* served as a self-designation within the Pachomian community, its linkage to the notion of community did not derive initially from the Pachomian definition of *koinōnia*, nor is it likely that it ever became throughout Egypt exclusively a technical term for a Pachomian form of community. It is important to underscore this fact lest the later references to *apotaktikoi* in the Coptic documentary papyri be read automatically as references to monks who practiced a Pachomian form of communal ascesis.

Apotaktikoi and the Renunciation of Property

The term *apotaktikos*, connected in the above discussion in Egypt with the communal ascetic life, derives from the Greek word *apotassō* which meant initially "to set apart" or "to appoint." In the course of time and certainly by the turn of the eras, it came to include the sense of removal or exclusion which, when directed towards the self, translates as renunciation (Rothenhaesler and Oppenheim; LSJ s.v.; Lampe s.v.). Its significance in early Christian circles drew from its use in Luke 14:33, where a disciple is defined as one who is able to give up or renounce all of his possessions (*apotassetai pasin tois autois heautou huparchousin*). Together with the demand to leave behind one's earthly family, which occurs but seven verses earlier (Luke 14:26), this section of the gospel became a *crux interpretationis* for early Christian ascetic practice and later monastic development.

The Lukan passage, especially when read alongside such gospel accounts as Jesus' call for the rich young man to sell all that he had and give to the poor (Matt 19:21), is easily interpreted as a call for the renunciation of ownership of private property. The monk, as the disciple before him, was to renounce all possessions. He was to live like the birds of the air and the beasts of the field, like Adam and Eve before the fall, and like the angels today (Frank), all of whom depend(ed) solely on God for their well-being. The literary accounts of Egyptian monasticism which proclaim this ideal are filled with stories of the renunciation of property and possessions by the movement's elite.[12] The influential *Vita Antonii* reports that its hero, following the gospel precept, sold his inheritance and distributed the proceeds to the poor before he embarked on his ascetic career (*Vita Antonii* 1–3). The anchoritic oriented sayings of the *Apophthegmata Patrum* indicate that while private property was not forbidden, it was scorned and purposefully kept to a minimum (Heussi: 251–54). Monks who received inheritances from relatives in the outside world were informed by their spiritual fathers of the dangers to the ascetic life inherent in them, and rejection of such gifts was strongly advocated.[13] Propertyless poverty became the literary ideal, expressed most beautifully and simply in the account of Apa Serapion, who sold his only possession, a gospel, and gave the proceeds to the poor, precisely because it had daily proclaimed to him the need to "sell all that you have and give to the poor."[14]

It remained initially, however, an ideal, since an ascetic life required a minimal amount of property—a cell, clothing, objects to trade for food, etc. (Goehring, 1990b).

It was the innovation of the Pachomian movement that first appears to have offered the individual monk a means to fulfill completely the gospel demand to renounce *all* of one's personal property. Such personal renunciation was fulfilled though the act of contributing one's belongings to the monastery. The *Praecepta* of the Pachomian *Regula* require prospective members to renounce their parents and their possessions (*Praecepta* 49; Boon: 25–26; Veilleux: 2.153), and a catechesis attributed to Theodore speaks matter of factly of those who renounced their possessions to embark on a monastic career (ⲁⲩⲱ ⲛ̄ⲥⲉⲁⲡⲟⲧⲁⲥⲥⲉ ⲛ̄ⲛⲉⲩⲛ̄ⲕⲁ ⲉⲡⲓⲧⲟⲟⲧⲙ; Lefort, 1956:49.23; Veilleux: 3.105). When Petronius convinced his father to join him in the Pachomian community, the latter brought with him to the monastery "everything he had: cattle, sheep, and all sorts of gear, and he donated it to the community" (*G1* 80 = *Bo* 56; translation from Veilleux: 1.352). Shenoute likewise required prospective monks to donate their belongings to the monastery and devised a written document to insure the legal basis of the transfer (Leipoldt: 106–16; Krause, 1985:123).[15] The literary evidence of the early Pachomian and Shenoutean systems corresponds well with the demand in the Justinian code that the possessions of a person entering a monastery become *ex lege* the property of the monastery (Steinwenter, 1958:24; Krause, 1985:124; MacCoull, 1988:44–45).

Certainly the success of the Pachomian and Shenoutean communities depended in part on this innovation. It permitted the fulfillment of the letter of the gospel through the renunciation of *all* personal property at the same time that it met the ascetic's basic need for food, clothing and shelter through the property and wealth of the monastery. The question remains, however, whether such innovation was a universal aspect of communal monasticism in Egypt, or whether it was limited to certain monastic communities. To answer this question, one must return to the evidence of the *apotaktikoi*, which, as has been shown above, served in Egypt as a label indicating an individual's involvement in communal ascetic practice.

The growing corpus of fourth-century Greek documentary papyri that refer to *apotaktikoi(ai)* (Judge, 1981: 613–20; Wipszycka: 625–36; Emmett: 510–13) offer relatively clear evidence that some monks so titled could own property. As was noted above, in those cases where an *apotaktikos* is recorded as paying tax on land (P. Berl. inv. 11860; P. Herm. Land.), it is possible that the land was owned by the monk's monastery; such was indeed the case in P. Berl. inv. 11860. In the archive of Apa Johannes (P. Herm. 7–10), Johannes, who is called both *anachōrētēs* and *apotaktikos*, is reported to have taken money (8 solidi) for his service of obtaining the letter writer's release from military service.[16] One could also preserve the propertyless state of the *anachōrētēs-apotaktikos* here by assuming that the money taken in by Apa Johannes belonged to the larger community of which he was a part, but that goes beyond the evidence of the letters.

Other documents supply more conclusive evidence. A text dated to 381 CE (P. Lips. 28) records the entrusting of her grandson by a woman at Hermopolis to his uncle Silvanus, an *apotaktikos*, who promises in turn to hold the child's inheritance until the child comes of age and to make the child heir to his own estate. Here there seems to be little doubt that an *apotaktikos* did own property.[17] A second document, a lease agreement of 400 CE (P. Oxy. XLIV 3203), records the lease of a portion of a house in Oxyrhynchus to a Jew by two natural sisters, Theodora and Tauris, *monachai apotaktikai*. The personal ownership of the house by these two female *apotaktikai* seems clear.

A final text (P. Oxy. XLVI 3311; 373–374 CE) is particularly illuminating. It is a legal document in which two sisters petition to regain control of property that their paternal cousin willed to his natural uncle, Ammonios, an *apotaktikos*. Ammonios has subsequently died, and the property is being held by a certain Ammon, whom the sisters claim is neither a son nor an heir.[18] While the Ammon in question may be a fellow *apotaktikos* who has retained Ammonios' inheritance for the community (Judge, 1981:618–19), there is no question but that the cousin had willed it originally to the individual *apotaktikos*, Ammonios. As such, the sisters' legal claim is that the title to the inheritance, in view of the absence of a will, should revert to them, i.e. it should remain in the natural family.

It must therefore be concluded that in the fourth century the term *apotaktikos* did not, in and of itself, indicate the status of the person so labeled as propertied or propertyless (cf. Krause, 1985: 122; Elm: 198). While the Pachomians, self-styled *apotaktikoi*, did not own property as individuals, the papyri discussed above indicate that other *apotaktikoi* did, as individuals, retain ownership of personal property. If we assume that such *apotaktikoi* lived in some form of community, then we must conclude that not all ascetic communities required their members to renounce their personal property. The Pachomian innovation of donating personal property to the monastery was not universal among communal ascetics in fourth-century Egypt.

This view is confirmed in the growing documentary evidence of Melitian monastic communities in Egypt. The sources include two sales contracts dated to 512–513 CE (SB I 5174–75; Sayce), an archive of texts from the 330s connected with the Melitian monastery of Hathor (P. Lond. 1913–1922; Bell, 1924:38–99), and the archive of Nepheros, dated slightly later in the fourth century and also deriving from a monastery of Hathor, presumably to be equated with the monastery of Hathor in P. Lond. 1913–1922 (Kramer and Shelton).[19] While the term *apotaktikos* does not appear with certainty in any of these texts,[20] their communal organization and the fact that individual members could retain personal property seems clear.

The two sales contracts (SB I 5174–75) record the sale of two groups of monastic cells that existed within the Melitian monastery of Labla in the vicinity of Arsinoë. The cells belonged to a certain Eulogius who apparently came into their possession when he was a Melitian monk in the Labla monastery. He is selling the cells because he has since left the Melitian community and joined the orthodox monastery of Mikrou Phyon in the same vicinity.[21] When one turns to the earlier documents contained in the archive of Nepheros, the individual ownership of property is again underlined. The texts include references to a monk who owns a small piece of land, to one who sold a house and inherited a weaving workshop, and to one who made loans at interest (Kramer and Shelton: 18). Finally, the earliest materials (P. Lond. 1913–22), while they do not contain any clear references to private ownership, do indicate considerable economic activity. Furthermore, it is possible that the main figure in this archive, Apa Paieous, not only headed, but owned the community under his control (Hengstenberg, 1927: 140–41; cf. Steinwenter, 1930).

Other documents offer evidence for the continuing practice of private property ownership within various Egyptian monasteries. A Greek text of 589 CE from Apollonos Polis (P. Köln 157; Hagedorn; Krause, 1985:124) records the emancipation of a slave by the monk Victor of the monastery of Apa Macrobius. Since emancipation requires previous ownership, the text once again affirms private ownership within a monastery setting. Among the papers of the sixth-century lawyer from Aphrodito, Dioscoros, one finds documents that make arrangements for certain monks entering a monastery to inherit property from their mother (MacCoull, 1985; 1988:36–47). An eighth-century document from Jeme, which preserves the only surviving application for admission to a monastery, makes no mention of the applicant's renunciation of his property or its donation to the monastery, in obvious distinction from the Pachomian and Shenutean practices (Crum, 1939b:9–10; Krause, 1985:124). Finally, five documents (BM Or. 6201–6204, 6206) edited by Martin Krause (1958; 1985:126–28) record the purchase and sale of specific cell groups within a larger monastery by individual monks, three of whom are distinctly identified as *apotaktikoi* (ⲁⲡⲟⲧⲁⲕⲧⲓⲕⲟⲥ ⲙ̅ⲙⲟⲛⲁⲭⲟⲥ).

These texts date from the ninth century (833–850 CE) and derive from the non-Pachomian monastery of Apollo at Bawit (Krause, 1958; 1966; 1985:126; Coquin and Martin; Torp). They clearly illustrate that in the ninth century in certain communities individual *apotaktikoi* could possess their own money with which to purchase their own cell(s).[22] The situation is complicated in these later texts by the fact that in certain monasteries individual monks could turn money over to the central authority of the community to be held by the community until the individual monk had need of it (Krause, 1958:213–24).[23]

While additional late documents could be noted, the evidence for a continuity in the practice of private property ownership within certain monastic communities in Egypt seems clear. The question about the classification of these various monasteries naturally arises. The traditional answer is that those monasteries in which private property was permitted represent anchoritic communities[24] and should be carefully distinguished from full coenobitic communities such as those of Pachomius and Shenoute. Martin Krause rightly questioned the rigidity of this division with respect to the monastery of Apollo at Bawit, observing "dass wir das nach den Regeln Pachoms und Schenutes organisierte Klosterwesen nur aus den zwar reichen literarischen Quellen des 4. und 5. Jahrhunderts kennen" (1985:128). I would go further and argue that any sharp division between anchoritic and coenobitic communities in Egypt in general is best eliminated as a product of the impact of the literary sources. This is not to deny the significance of the Pachomian communal organization, but to recognize that in making it the defining model of communal monasticism on the basis of its literary success, we force all other models of communal asceticism into the anchoritic camp and lose thereby any sense of a continuum between the two (cf. Kramer and Shelton: 18–20).

It is better to accept a fluidity in the practice of communal ascetic organization in Egypt, a fluidity confirmed in the sources' own use of the term *apotaktikos*. As we have seen, it was used from the beginning both of monks who owned personal property and of those, like the Pachomians, who did not. It is not necessary to account for the later uses of the term with reference to communal monks who owned property by positing a shift in meaning brought on by changing times and the imposition of the poll tax on the monasteries (Krause, 1985:127–29; Bell, 1926:265–75). While in those communities that originally required their members to surrender all personal property such a shift in meaning may have occurred in later years through necessity, the evidence augurs against any notion of a more general shift in the meaning of the term throughout Egypt. There were after all various ascetic communities, e.g. those of the Melitians, where private property ownership had always been accepted. In such communities the notion of a shift in the meaning of *apotaktikos* to include the ownership of personal property is meaningless. In the case of the monastery of Apollo at Bawit where the documentary evidence indicates private property ownership in the ninth century, it is just as likely that the monks of this monastery had always been able to own property as it is that their original rule shifted in later years to allow it.

Apotaktikos: Meaning and History

In her recent study on "Female Ascetics in the Greek Papyri," Alanna Emmett held in her conclusion that "as monasticism developed, *apotaktikos* accumulated more usage but remained a term which drew a line between those who remained more or less in conformity with regular ways of handling family, property and other social ties and those who renounced customary patterns" (513). While the ideal of *apotaxis* might include total renunciation of family, possessions and social ties, practical reality surely led to different degrees and patterns of implementation. The use of the term *apotaktikos* thus indicated a person within the church who, on the basis of his or her Christian belief, renounced the traditional social patterns of Roman Egypt; it did not necessarily specify which patterns were renounced nor the degree to which they were renounced.

One suspects that the term *anachōrētēs* had originally a similar meaning within the church, namely, a person who withdrew, on the basis of Christian belief, from the traditional social responsibilities of Roman Egypt. Over time the term *anachōrētēs* came to indicate one who withdrew spatially from the community, a definition fostered in particular by Athanasius' *Vita Antonii* whose hero fled to the desert. It is possible that as this spatial element was emphasized in the definition of *anachōrētēs*, it propelled the meaning of the term more towards the idea of solitary withdrawal and its customary equation with the anchorite or hermit monk.

Apotaktikos, on the other hand, perhaps in part to compensate for the void left by the meaning of *anachōrētēs*, came to refer to those ascetic individuals who chose to live together in some form of community. It thus became the communal life that defined the *apotaktikos* in Egypt, though the organizational principles of that communal life could vary widely. The Coptic literary sources and late documentary evidence clearly indicate that this communal dimension to the term's definition remained in force at least through the ninth century. Thus, Emmett's final stage in her history of the meaning of *apotaktikos*—namely that "with the hardening of institutional forms and the spread of the terms *monachos* and then *monazon*, *apotaktikos* reasserted itself in a more specialized sense, with something of the original eremitic overtones emphasized,"—appears incorrect.[25]

It seems more likely that the apparent shift in the meaning of *apotaktikos* in an anchoritic or eremitic direction detected by Emmett is a result of the redefinition of Egyptian ascetic terminology for a non-Egyptian audience. In the more northern provinces, the term *apotaktikai* came to be associated with certain "heretical" groups. Basil of Caesarea, for example, in his second canonical letter (374–75 CE), calls for the rebaptism of *encratites, saccophores* and *apotaktites* (*Ep* 199; PG 32.729–32; cf. Lambert: 2615–16). Epiphanius, writing about 376 CE (*Panarion* 1.2.1; PG 41.1040–52), refers to a heretical sect in Phrygia, Cilicia and Pamphylia who term themselves *apostolikoi* or *apotaktikai* (Lambert: 2616; Judge, 1977:80). Given such developments outside of Egypt, it is no surprise that the general Egyptian use of the term *apotaktikos* for individuals practicing a communal ascetic life required careful translation in the literary presentation of Egyptian monasticism to the outside world. The importance of the issue is apparent in the transmission of the *Vita Pachomii*, where, while the term *apotaktikos* occurs with relative frequency in the Coptic recensions of the *vita*, it has disappeared from the Greek and Latin versions.[26] The latter, meant at least ultimately for a non-Egyptian audience,[27] deleted the term as incompatible with the literary orthodoxy of the Pachomian movement.

Perhaps the clearest and most influential example of this development occurs in the relabeling of the threefold division of ascetic practice current in Egypt. In two separate Coptic sources attributed to Athanasius and Pachomius respectively, the three types of ascetics noted in Egypt are the *parthenoi*, the *apotaktikoi*, and the *anachōrētai*. For the Egyptian audience, the terms denoted simply the various forms of ascetic life; they appear to have offered no information on the practitioner's position relative to theological issues. When Jerome reports the three forms of Egyptian ascetic practice to the Roman lady Eustochium, however, the terms become *coenobium, anachoretae* and *remnuoth*. Not only has the Egyptian term for the communal ascetic, *apotaktikoi*, been replaced by *coenobium* (or *coenobiotae* in Cassian, *Conf.* 18.4), but now the terms carry a theological dimension. The *anachoretae* and the *coenobium* represent the politically correct forms of the ascetic life, and the *remnuoth* are dismissed as heretics.

What is important to note is that the term by which we today most often describe an Egyptian communal ascetic, the term coenobite, was not the common term used to describe a communal monk in Egypt.[28] In its modern usage, it connects too readily with the literarily well-documented Pachomian community or self-styled *koinōnia*, and comes thereby to equate too simplistically Egyptian communal monasticism with its Pachomian form. The more diverse use of *apotaktikos* in the Egyptian sources argues for more diversity in the organizational forms of communal ascetic practice in Egypt.[29]

The continuing impact of Jerome's terminological shift is seen in the tendency to equate forms of Egyptian monastic life that do not at first glance fit the usual definitions of anchoritic and coenobitic monasticism (which are in fact Jerome's definitions) with Jerome's *remnuoth*. Judge made this move when he connected the papyrological evidence of the *apotaktikoi* with the *remnuoth*. Kramer and Shelton, in similar fashion, suggest that Melitian monasticism, as evidenced in the papyri, also fits Jerome's third category (18–20; cf. Hengstenberg, 1927: 141–42). While not denying the existence of monks who lived a life as Jerome describes that of the *remnuoth*, we must be careful not to allow his three-fold division to become a *sine qua non* for our understanding of Egyptian monasticism. It is probably not an accident that the *apotaktikoi* and the Melitian monks do not fit easily into the usual picture of Egyptian monasticism defined in anchoritic (Antonian) and coenobitic (Pachomian) terms. That is not sufficient reason, however, to equate them with the *remnuoth*. Evidence for both derives from non-literary papyrological sources which, as such, do not participate fully in the literary definitions of the monastic life. Rather than force them into the literary models by linking these "odd" monks with Jerome's *remnuoth*, we should question the literary models.

In his identification of the *apotaktikoi* of the papyri with the *remnuoth*, Judge accepted Jerome's terminological shift from *apotaktikoi* to *coenobium* as the label for communal ascetics in Egypt. As a result, the use of the term *apotaktikoi*, which in the Egyptian sources is most likely a simple reference to communal ascetics, with no specification of the organizational form of their community, becomes evidence of a third form of the ascetic life (the apotactic movement), a form probably not recognized, as such, in Egypt.[30] The theologically motivated imposition of a non-Egyptian terminology on the literary presentation of Egyptian monasticism outside of Egypt has come, not only here, but in general, to define the Egyptian movement. It is a false step. To understand Egyptian monasticism, we must listen to the Egyptians.

In terms of the impact of the literary models on our understanding of asceticism, it must be recognized that ascetic practice in Egypt was more diverse than the literary models indicate. This is true not only with reference to doctrine, but also with reference to practice. As the literary models of asceticism took hold in the minds of the early Christians, their rhetoric of *imitatio* not only forced the future into a prescribed mold, it also reshaped the past. Historically, the ascetic practice represented by the literary source is most at home in the later age that the source itself helped to shape. Documentary sources, on the other hand, do not present models of ascetic practice designed to shape the future or the past, but simply record examples of such practice. While their interpretation has its own methodological difficulties, they offer direct access to specific cases in specific ages and thus serve as a check against the ascetic models of the literary sources. They can never replace the literary sources, but they can help put them in perspective. The study of the technical terminology of asceticism offered above is but an attempt, through the use of such documentary evidence, to lift ever so slightly the literary veil.

NOTES

[1] The research for this study was conducted in 1989–90 at the Akademie der Wissenschaften in Göttingen, Germany under the auspices of the Alexander von Humboldt Stiftung.

[2] The Greek term *koinobion* is relatively common, but the use of *koinobiōtēs* is rare (Lampe, s.v.). In Coptic, while the loan word *koinōnia* is again relatively common, particularly in the Pachomian tradition, the term *koinobion* occurs much less frequently (Crum, 1939a: 692a). I have found no use of the form *koinobiōtēs* in Coptic. In Latin, the use of both *coenobium* and *coenobita* is more common (Blaise, s.v.), though judging from the manuscript tradition of Jerome's twenty-second letter, the use of *coenobita* was a secondary development (*Ep.* 22.34–35 in CSEL 54.196–97).

[3] One can only speculate as to why these "orthodox" church fathers favored the anchoritic and coenobitic forms of monasticism while discrediting so vehemently its urban variety. Perhaps it was precisely because the latter were less remote and hence more active in civil and religio-political issues. Such activity would come into direct conflict with the growing authority of the clergy and the bishops; cf. Rousseau.

[4] It is clear, however, from these churchmen's opposition to such monks, as well as from the secular criticism of them found in Julian (*Or.* 7.18; *Ep.* 89b) and Libanius (*Or.* 30.8; 2.32), that the more urban form of monasticism continued to exist (Judge, 1977:79–80).

[5] Jerome employs the term *coenobium* where one might expect *coenobitae*. He refers to *coenobium, quod illi sauhes gentili lingua uocant, nos in commune uiuentes possumus appellare* (*Ep.* 22.34) and *quos uocari coenobium diximus* (*Ep.* 22.35). Some later manuscripts emend the text so that the above citations read *coenobitae* and *coenobitas* respectively (CSEL 54.196–97). I have retained Jerome's use of *coenobium* when referring to his threefold division of Egyptian monasticism in this paper.

[6] The use of Jerome's and Cassian's three-fold categorization of Egyptian monasticism, while perhaps applicable in a broad sense, drastically oversimplifies the variety of ascetic practice in Egypt. Not only does the presentation stand monastic history on its head by placing the earliest form (*remnuoth* or *sarabaitae*) last (Hengstenberg, 1935:355–62), it tends to foster general definitions for anchoritic and coenobitic monasticism. Such definitions in turn serve to identify all monks under one or the other "descriptive" label and thus blur differentiations within the individual categories.

[7] The latter assumption illustrates the impact of the Pachomian model on the current understanding of Egyptian communal monasticism.

[8] Judge (1977: 83) recognizes the problem of these texts for his thesis and seeks to solve it by suggesting that Apa Johannes, the anchorite, "may not have been so far removed from the position of Jerome's worldly *remnuoth*, and the addressing of him as *apotaktikos* may be a better index of his position in the civil community." Be that as it may, the overlap of the terms is nonetheless apparent.

A. Emmett (512) suggests, since Apa Johannes terms himself *anachōrētēs* while he is addressed by another as *apotaktikos*, that the former term is internal to the monastic society while the latter term, *apotaktikos*, is used externally. This fits with the use of *apotaktikos* in other legal documents where, as Emmett shows, it more clearly identified the figure to the outsider than did the label *anachōrētēs*, which had wide currency in Egypt and carried considerable legal meaning in terms of the evasion of one's civic responsibilities. *Anachōrētēs*, in its monastic meaning, occurs most often internally within monastic sources. It should be noted, however, that the other use of the term *anachōrētēs* in the archive of Apa Johannes is in a letter addressed to Johannes, i.e., external.

[9] It will be argued below that the *apotaktikoi* should not be equated with Jerome's *remnuoth*, but rather, at least in some of its manifestations, with the group that Jerome labels *coenobium*. But even when we accept that shift, the image of Apa Johannes overlaps Jerome's categories.

[10] Judge's analysis likewise supports a communal element in the meaning of the term (1977:85).

[11] Another late fourth century letter (SB VIII.1 9683) also mentions *anachōrētai* living in a *monē* (Emmett: 512).

[12] The literary *topos* should be seen in part as the expression of a radical norm which functions to maintain group identity. Cf. Pokorny: 112–18.

[13] *Apophthegmata Patrum*, Poemen 33 (PG 65.329D-332A), Arsenius 29 (PG 65.97B-C). Arsenius refused an inheritance from a senator who had died by noting that he had died to the world long before the senator's death. Cf. *Historia Lausiaca* 14.2 and 61.4.

[14] *Apophthegmata Patrum*, anonymous collection, book 3, saying 70 (English translation in Waddell: 140); cf. *Apophthegmata Patrum*, Theodore of Pherme 1 (PG 65.188A).

[15] For an example of an inheritance given to a monk and later disputed by secular relatives, see P. Oxy. XLVI 3311.

[16] Johannes fits well the pattern of the patron noted by Peter Brown (1971:80–131). It is interesting to note that the author writes to Johannes to get his money back, since Johannes was apparently unsuccessful in obtaining the writer's release from military service.

[17] This text raises the further question of the extent to which the monastic ideal of renunciation of one's earthly family was actually carried out in practice.

[18] The editor of the text, Rea (96–98), suggests that Ammon was indeed next of kin and heir to Ammonios and that the sisters were simply arguing that the latter was never really the full legal owner of the estate.

[19] It must be noted that the monastery of Hathor in the P. Lond. 1913–22 archive is situated in the upper Cynopolite nome, while that of the Nepheros archive is said to be in the Hermopolite nome. Kramer and Shelton (11–15) argue convincingly nonetheless for the equation of the two sites.

[20] The one possible use of the term appears only as a result of textual emendation. It is certainly not clear that the lacuna should be so reconstructed (Kramer and Shelton: 44, note to line 12–13).

[21] It is interesting to note that the *postophoroi* of the Egyptian temples of the Greco-Roman period lived in rooms or *postophoria* within the temple, which they purchased and owned. An individual *postophoros* could, moreover, own more than one *postophorion*. While the *postophorion* could be willed to an heir, proceeds from its sale apparently went to the state (Evans: 194–95, 205).

[22] According to a clause in the documents, a cell could not be left to relatives or others outside of the monastery, but reverted on the death of the individual to the diakonia of the monastery (Krause, 1985:127). This was, however, not always the case. P. Oxy. XVI 1891 records that a certain Serena inherited a milling-bakery from the monk Copreous, which she in turn leased to a baker and his son. The bakery was located in the monastery of Apa Copreous in the western desert of the city.

23 Wipszycka (634) considered this theory *"très fragile,"* but the Coptic evidence is certainly there to support the existence of the practice (e.g. CLT 1 and 2; Krause, 1985:132-33, n. 81; Schiller: 16-33).

24 The anchoritic community is best represented by the communities in the Wadi Natrun. They are seen to parallel to an extent the lavra pattern in Palestine. Note that the Melitian texts, SN I 5174-75, refer to a monastery of Labla, which Hengstenberg (1935:357) already connected with the term lavra.

25 Emmett's conclusions are based on the earlier Greek documentary evidence.

26 Compare the Bohairic text wherein Apa Psahref informs the investigating Duke Artemios that "we are *apotaktikoi* (ⲀⲚⲞⲚ ϨⲀⲚⲢⲰⲘⲒ ⲚⲀⲠⲞⲦⲀⲔⲦⲒⲔⲞⲤ; Lefort, 1925:166.10-11) with the Greek *Vita prima* version where the line drops out (Halkin: 87).

27 While early Greek forms of the *vita* may have originated in Egypt, they survive today in later non-Egyptian manuscripts.

28 Jerome notes (*Ep.* 22.34) that the *coenobium* are called *sauhes* in Egypt. *Sauhes* is the Coptic ⲤⲞⲞⲨϨⲤ which is used of monastic communities or monks residing in them, though not exclusively of the Pachomian variety (Crum, 1939a:s.v.). The Coptic recensions of the *Vita Pachomii* refer to the *koinōnia* and employ the verb *koinōnein*; they refer to the monks, however, as *apotaktikoi* and *monachoi*.

29 The archeology of various monastic sites suggests a similar diversity (cf., Grossmann; Krause 1966; Coquin and Martin; Torp).

30 This is not to deny some form of urban monasticism as posited by Judge, but rather to question the identification of the term *apotaktikoi* with individuals who practiced that form. One doubts that the term had any connection with the geographic location of one's ascetic enterprise.

WORKS CONSULTED

Bell, H. Idris
    1924   *Jews and Christians in Egypt: The Jewish Troubles in Alexandria and the Athanasian Controversies*. London: The British Museum; rpt. Westport, CN: Greenwod, 1972.

    1926   "Two Official Letters of the Arab Period." *Journal of Egyptian Archaeology* 12:265-81.

Blaise, Albert
    1954   *Dictionnaire latin–français des auteurs chrétiens*. Turnhout: Éditions Brepols.

Boon, Amand
    1932   *Pachomiana latine. Règle et épitres de s. Pachome, épitre de s. Théodore et "liber" de s. Orsiesius. Text latin de s. Jerome*. Bibliothèque de la revue d'histoire ecclésiastique 7. Louvain: Bureaux de la revue.

Brown, Peter
    1971   "The Rise and Function of the Holy Man in Late Antiquity." *JRS* 61:80-131.

1988 *The Body and Society. Men, Women and Sexual Renunciation in Early Christianity.* New York: Columbia University Press.

Coquin, René-Georges and Maurice Martin
1991 "Bawit: History." Pp. 363–63 in *The Coptic Encyclopedia,* vol. 2. Ed. Aziz S. Atiya. New York: Macmillan.

Crum, Walter E.
1939a *A Coptic Dictionary.* Oxford: Clarendon Press.
1939b *Varia Coptica. Texts, Translations, Indexes.* Aberdeen: University Press.

Elm, Susanna K.
1986 "The Organization and Institutions of Female Asceticism in Fourth Century Cappadocia and Egypt." Dissertation. Oxford University.

Emmett, Alanna
1982 "Female Ascetics in the Greek Papyri." Pp. 507–15 in *XVI Internationaler Byzantinistenkongress Wien, 4.–9. Oktober 1981,* Akten II Teil. Ed. Wolfram Hörander, et al. Jahrbuch der österreichischen Byzantinik 23,2. Wien: Der österreichischen Akademie der Wissenschaften.

Evans, J. A. S.
1961 *A Social and Economic History of an Egyptian Temple in the Greco-Roman Period.* Yale Classical Studies 17. New Haven: Yale University Press.

Frank, K. Suso
1964 *ΑΓΓΕΛΙΚΟΣ ΒΙΟΣ. Begriffsanalytische und begriffsgeschichtliche Untersuchung zum "Engelgleichen Leben" im frühen Mönchtum.* Beitrag zur Geschichte des alten Mönchtums und des Benediktinerordens 26. Münster–Westfalen: Aschendorff.

Goehring, James E.
1986 "New Frontiers in Pachomian Studies." Pp. 236–57 in *The Roots of Egyptian Christianity.* Ed. Birger A. Pearson and James E. Goehring. Studies in Antiquity and Christianity 1. Philadelphia: Fortress.
1990a "Theodore's Entry into the Pachomian Movement (Selections from the Life of Pachomius)." Pp. 349–56 in *Ascetic Behavior in Greco–Roman Antiquity: A Sourcebook.* Ed. Vincent L. Wimbush. Studies in Antiquity and Christianity. Minneapolis: Fortress.

1990b   "The World Engaged. The Social and Economic World of Early Egyptian Monasticism." Pp. 134–44 in *Gnosticism & the Early Christian World: In Honor of James M. Robinson*. Ed. James E. Goehring, et al. Sonoma, CA: Polebridge.

Grossmann, Peter
1986   "Die Unterkunftsbauten des Koinobitenklosters 'Dair al-Balayza' im Vergleich mit dem Eremitagen der Mönche von Kellia." Pp. 33–40, fig. 2 in *Le site monastique copte des Kellia. Sources historiques et explorations archéologiques. Actes du Colloque de Genève, 13 au 15 aout 1984*. Genève: Mission suisse d'archéologie copte de l'Université de Genève.

Hagedorn, Dieter
1980   "Sklavenfreilassung." Pp. 150–61 in *Kölner Papyri (P. Köln)*. Ed. Bärbel Kramer, et al. Papyrologica Coloniensia 7. Opladen: Westdeutscher Verlag.

Halkin, François
1932   *S. Pachomii Vitae Graecae*. Subsidia hagiographica 19. Bruxelles: Société des Bollandistes.

Haslam, M. W.
1976   "3203. Lease of Exedra and Cellar." Pp. 182–84 in *The Oxyrhynchus Papyri*, vol XLIV. Ed. A. K. Bowman, et al. London: Egypt Exploration Society.

Hengstenberg, Wilhelm
1927   Review of H. Idris Bell, *Jews and Christians in Egypt. Byzantinische Zeitschrift* 27:138–45.
1935   "Bemerkungen zur Entwicklungsgeschichte des ägyptischen Mönchtums." *Bulletin de l'Institut archéologique bulgare* 9:355–62 = *Actes du IVe Congrès international des études byzantines*. Ed. Bogdan D. Filou. Sophia: Imprimerie de la Cour.

Heussi, Karl
1936   *Der Ursprung des Mönchtums*. Tübingen: Mohr; rpt., Aalen: Scientia, 1981.

Judge, E. A.
1977   "The Earliest Use of Monachos for 'Monk' (P. Coll. Youtie 77) and the Origins of Monasticism." *JAC* 10:72–89.
1981   "Fourth–Century Monasticism in the Papyri." Pp. 613–20 in *Proceedings of the Sixteenth International Congress of Papyrology,*

New York, 24–32 July 1990. Ed. Roger S. Bagnall, et al. American Studies in Papyrology 23. Chico, CA: Scholars Press.

Kramer, Bärbel and John C. Shelton
1987   *Das Archiv des Nepheros und verwandte Texte.* Aegyptiaca Treverensia 4. Mainz am Rhein: Philipp von Zabern.

Krause, Martin
1958   "Das Apa-Apollo-Kloster zu Bawit. Untersuchungen unveröffentlichter Urkunden als Beitrag zur Geschichte des ägyptischen Mönchtums." Dissertation. Karl-Marx-Universität, Leipzig.
1966   "Bawit." Pp. 568–83 in *Reallexikon zur byzantinischen Kunst,* vol. 1. Ed. Klaus Wessel. Stuttgart: Hiersemann.
1985   "Zur Möglichkeit von Besitz im apotaktischen Mönchtums Ägyptens." Pp. 121–33 in *Acts of the Second International Congress of Coptic Studies, Roma, 22–26 September 1980.* Ed. Tito Orlandi and Frederik Wisse. Rome: CIM.

Lambert, A.
1907   "Apotactites et Apotaxamènes." Cols. 2604–26 in *Dictionnaire d'archéologie chrétienne et de liturgie,* vol. 1. Ed. Fernand Cabrol. Paris: Letouzey et Ané.

Lampe, G. W. H.
1961   *A Patristic Greek Lexicon.* Oxford: Clarendon.

Lantshoot, A. van
1927   "Lettre de saint Athanase au sujet de l'amour et de la tempérence." *Le Muséon* 40:265–92.

Lefort, L. Th.
1921   "La règle de S. Pachôme (étude d'approche)." *Le Muséon* 34:61–70.
1925   *S. Pachomii vita bohairice scripta.* CSCO 89. Paris: e typographeo reipublicae; rpt., Louvain: Secrétariat du Corpus SCO, 1965.
1933   *S. Pachomii vitae sahidice scriptae.* CSCO 99/100. Paris: e typographeo reipublicae; rpt., Louvain: Secrétariat du Corpus SCO, 1965.
1956   *Oeuvres de S. Pachôme et de ses disciples.* CSCO 159 (text) and 160 (translation). Louvain: L. Durbecq.

Leipoldt, Johannes
1933   *Schenute von Atripe und die Entstehung des national ägyptischen Christentums.* Leipzig: Hinrichs.

MacCoull, Leslie S. B.
 1985 "A Coptic Session of Land by Dioscorus of Aphrodito: Alexandria Meets Cairo." Pp. 159–64 in *Acts of the Second International Congress of Coptic Studies, Roma, 22–26 September 1980*. Ed. Tito Orlandi and Frederik Wisse. Rome: CIM.
 1988 *Dioscorus of Aphrodito: His Works and His World*. The Transformation of the Classical Heritage 16. Berkeley: University of California Press.

Maraval, Pierre
 1982 *Égérie. Journal de voyage (Itinéraire)*. SC 296. Paris: Éditions du Cerf.

Pokorny, Petr
 1990 "Strategies of Social Formation in the Gospel of Luke." Pp. 106–18 in *Gospel Origins and Christian Beginnings: In Honor of James M. Robinson*. Ed. James E. Goehring, et al. Sonoma, CA: Polebridge.

Rea, J. R.
 1978 *The Oxyrhynchus Papyri*, vol. 46. London: Egypt Exploration Society.

Rothenhaeusler, M. and P. Oppenheim
 1950 "Apotaxis." *RAC* 1:558–64.

Rousseau, Philip
 1978 *Ascetics, Authority, and the Church in the Age of Jerome and Cassian*. Oxford: Oxford University Press.

Rubenson, Samuel
 1990 *The Letters of St. Antony: Origenist Theology, Monastic Tradition and the Making of a Saint*. Bibliotheca Historico-ecclesiastica Lundensis 24. Lund: Lund University Press.

Sayce, A. H.
 1890 "Deux contrats grecs du fayoum." *Revue des études grecques* 3:131–44.

Schiller, A. Arthur
 1932 *Ten Coptic Legal Texts*. New York: The Metropolitan Museum of Art.

Steinwenter, Artur
  1930 "Die Rechtsstellung der Kirchen un Klöster nach der Papyri." *Zeitschrift der Savigny-Stiftung für Rechtsgeschichte* 50, Kanonistisch Abteilung 19:1–50.
  1958 "Aus dem kirchlichen Vermögensrechte der Papyri." *Zeitschrift der Savigny-Stiftung für Rechtsgeschichte* 75, Kanonistische Abteilung 44:1–34.

Torp, Hjalmar
  1981 "Le monastère copte de Baouit. Quelques notes d'introduction." Pp. 1–8 in *Acta ad archaeologiam et artium historiam pertinentia*. Ed. Hjalmar Torp, et al. Miscellanea Coptica 9. Rome: Giorgio Bretschneider.

Veilleux, Armand
  1980–82 *Pachomian Koinonia*, 3 vols. Cistercian Studies Series 45–47. Kalamazoo, MI: Cistercian.

Waddell, Helen
  1957 *The Desert Fathers*. Ann Arbor: University of Michigan Press.

Wipszycka, Ewa
  1975 "Les terres de la congrégation pachômienne dans une liste de payments pour les apora." Pp. 625–36 in *Le monde grec, pensé, littérature, histoire, documents. Hommages à Claire Préaux*. Ed. J. Bingen, et al. Bruxelles: L'Université Bruxelles.

DAEMONS AND THE PERFECTING OF THE MONK'S BODY: MONASTIC ANTHROPOLOGY, DAEMONOLOGY, AND ASCETICISM[1]

Richard Valantasis
St. Louis University

ABSTRACT

Daemons contribute to the perfection of the monk's body. Although the traditional understanding constructs daemons as negative, in monastic asceticism they perform an important function. Asceticism relates to bodily transformation; therefore, the relation of the daemons to the monk's body assists the monk both in locating the passions to be stilled and in providing the appropriate arena of ascetical development. The understanding of daemonology, then, is not as forces exterior to the self, but as elements closely aligned with the formation and manipulation of the body itself. As a result of both the monastic anthropology and the monastic daemonology, monastic asceticism takes on another form, namely, to assist the monk in creating a new, angelic body which is stilled and transformed. This transformation can only occur with the help of the daemons who have become the monk's constant companion in a life of withdrawal.

The Problem—Daemons:

Daemons[2] are ubiquitous characters in monastic literature because monastic formation revolves about a struggle with them. Without the daemons, there could be no progress in the monastic life since progress begins when the daemons attack and succeeds by the monk's activity in their defeat. *Ascesis*, the metaphor chosen by the monks to describe their formation, itself implies such athletic contending with opponents: the metaphor requires some "contender" for its completion.

Our knowledge and understanding of daemons, however, emerges from a conflation of a number of discourses which include daemons. In addition to monastic ascetical daemonology (Harpham), studies of daemons intersect with studies of evil. The history of theodicy (Russell, 1987, 1981, 1984, 1988), witchcraft, and magic (Kelly) include daemons as major characters, while contemporary Jungian psychology (Jung) and Christian healing (Kelsey, 1978, 1973)—themselves relating to ancient texts—have emphasized the daemonic aspect of human illness and recovery. Moreover, daemons are part of the philosophical and theological discourse of antiquity (See "Démon"): Stoics and Platonists (Dodds, 1951:289–291) developed sophisticated daemonic theories to explain both cosmology and the human constitution (Dodds, 1965: ch. 2; Burkert: 179–181; Ferguson: 184–6 and 361–62). Finally, daemons have been incorporated into the mythic narrative structures (both biblical and cultural) of the primordial fall of human beings from an original good state as well as into the various narratives about Satan, the Devil, Lucifer, and fallen angels (Foerster). Each of these three sorts of discourses construct a peripheral daemonology and these peripheral constructions are then applied to monastic asceticism. In monastic ascetical literature, daemons seem to be different from all of these, but the interrelationship of daemons and monks in ascetical living remains problematic and difficult to isolate. The following saying of Amma Theodora illustrates this complexity:

> And again she said: "Not asceticism, neither vigils nor all sorts of toil, saves, except genuine humility. For there was a certain anchorite who drove out daemons [*apelaynōn daimonas*]. And he examined them: 'By what means do you come out [*en tini exerchesthai*]? By fasting?' And they said, 'We neither eat nor drink.' 'By vigils?' And they said, 'We do not sleep.' 'By withdrawal?' And they said, 'We dwell in the desert.' 'So by what means do you come out?' And they said, 'Nothing, except humility, conquers us.' Know that humility is conquerer of the daemons" (Amma Theodora, Saying 6).

In this interaction it is clear that the daemons and the monks have a geographical relationship since they both live in the desert. They both also practice the same ascetical discipline: withdrawal from society, limiting of food and drink, and vigils. That the daemons and the monks converse, and that the daemons are a subject of conversation among monks, indicates that they have a social relationship in which they converse with each other honestly and with respect. But they are locked in a discourse of power: daemons, despite their ascetical agility and proficiency, may be made "to come out from" (*exerchomai*) the monk who has the capacity to expel them (*apolaynō*) by having achieved "humility," and so the contest is between the daemons' advantage while within the monk, and the monk's advantage developed through asceticism.

For Amma Theodora, and in monastic literature generally, three systems interrelate: the system defining the "monk" as a category superior to "human being"; the system defining the daemons and their ethical signification; and the system explaining the relationship of monk and daemons in the ascetical life.

The monk (both as giver and receiver of ascetical teaching), however, is the invisible character in this dialogue. In our modern thinking (which we have projected onto the past), monks are simply "human beings" who live a particular "life-style." We assume that there exists an objective category "human being" which has perdured throughout all history, so that what a sixth-century monk means by "body" or "person" is the same as our contemporary understanding of human personality (Haraway;

Geertz: 33–54). We also assume that this universal "human being" moves into different totally exterior and independent social situations in which the "body" remains the same and only its accidental circumstances change (Michie: 3–11, 124–150; Rouselle: 1–62). Daemons have, then, been understood simply as a form of "primitive" psychology and the discussion of daemons in ascetic literature as the means of communicating primitive psychological insights about eternal, and historically non-determined, "psychological realities" (Nouwen; Jones). Scholars have only recently begun to explore the social construction of human embodiment and personality. It is generally recognized now that the "body," as well as the "person," is a social construction whose signification is neither given nor transparent. Monastic literature differentiates between "human being" and "monk." Although the monks often discuss the signification and condition of their being a "human being," they categorize themselves as "humans becoming angels" or "divine beings" or any number of similar descriptions. They experience themselves outside the primary category "human." The socially constructed concept "human being" becomes in a monastic culture "monk" and we cannot presume that the cultural signification and meaning of "monk" and "human" were the same.

This study will address each of these three categories of experience, monk, daemon, and asceticism, as complex metaphoric systems.[3] The foundation for understanding daemons in monastic asceticism is monastic anthropology. The first part of this study will attempt to construct the cultural systems which undergird the monk's own understanding of the body by noting what functions and meanings are assigned to the human body as distinct from other bodies (angelic and daemonic, animal), by tabulating the events that occur in and around the body, and by noting the kinds of socialized bodies available in the culture (married, virgin, celibate, cenobitic).

The daemonic forces operate within the framework of monastic anthropology. The second part of this study will gather information about daemons: their characteristics, origin, functions, social organizations, social relationships and effects upon human beings.

Monastic asceticism employs an anthropology and a daemonology in a program of self-improvement. The third part of this study will explore monastic asceticism as a metaphorical system of perfection through daemonic transformation, which constitutes the transformation and perfection of the monk's body.

Part One: Monastic Anthropology

The Social Body

Recent studies of pagan and Christian *anachōrēsis* have accustomed us to think in social categories when defining the monk's life (Fowden; Kirschner). Peter Brown (1988:5–36) has demonstrated that the body in Late Antiquity belonged to society and the city and, therefore, was inscribed with political responsibility: "If their little world was not to come to an end for lack of citizens, they must reproduce it, every generation, by marriage, intercourse and the begetting and rearing of children" (Brown, 1988:7). I would contend not that the body belonged to society or that it primarily bore social significance (as does Brown), but rather that the monk's body consisted of all its social relationships. The body itself was defined by its social environment. What to our mind is a "scientific," or medically defined, body engaged in social relationships was for the monks a series of different social bodies defined by the social environment in which those bodies lived. The society, developed from the intricate relations of socially embodied people, belonged to the body, not the body to society. Such an observation is critical to understanding the next section on monastic anthropology because what we would call the scientific body also consisted of a social and communal dimension.

The socialized body of the monk becomes even more complex in its social dimension. Even though the monk claimed to have withdrawn from society, political life and even the Church (Brown, 1988:213–84), the monk's self-definition was based upon a complex system of social distinctions involving the monk's differentiation between human beings, monks, angels, daemons, other types of human being, and other manners of social life. The monk, thus, creates a social identity by defining the self in relation to other creatures (angels and daemons), as well as by defining the social self in relation to other social groups (the married, the chaste, city-dwellers, desert-dwellers, the coenobium). Each of these two foci of self-definition (other creatures and other social groups) will be taken up serially.

Self-definition in relation to other creatures:

The monk's social definition rests on a primary and fundamental distinction between angels, daemons and human beings. The differentiation of one from the other revolves about two essential categories: those creatures who are capable of falling (*piptō*); those creatures who are capable of rising up (*anistēmi, egeirō*):

> It is the property of angels . . . not to fall, and even, as some say, it is quite impossible for them to fall. It is the property of men to fall and to rise again as often as this may happen. But it is the property of devils (*daimonōn*), and devils alone, not to rise once they have fallen (John Climacus, *Ladder*, Step IV, Moore #31, PG 696D).

Both the capacity to fall and the capacity to rise are based on two interlocking assumptions: the priority of higher over lower, and of stability over movement (Williams, 1981; 1985). The ability to ascend or be raised up determines an ascending hierarchy in which the human being functions in an intermediate state between daemons and angels, sharing with daemons the ability to fall, and exhibiting a capacity for rising upward toward those beings who cannot fall. The solidarity between the fallen beings (humans and daemons) masks the particular status of angels who neither fall, nor do they consequently need to rise again. Human movability highlights the immovability of both daemons (who cannot rise) and angels (who do not fall). Humanity, here, is that creature capable of falling, like the daemons, and capable of rising toward the higher creatures, the angels.[4]

Mirroring the distinction between angel, human, and daemon is a distinction made about kinds of human being. Human beings are categorized by their ability to live virtuously: those who are evil, those who are a mixture of evil and good, and those who are good. Such categorizations of evil, mixed, and good are frequent in ascetic literature (both monastic and gnostic). There is a long tradition of distinction between the psychic and the pneumatic person: for example, 1 Cor 3:1–4; and also people categorized as hylic, psychic, and pneumatic (for example, both the structure of the scriptures and their implied readership in *The Letter to Flora* (Epiphanius, *Panarion* 33.3.1—33.7.10; text in Layton 306–315; see also Pagels, 1986; Rudolph: 88–113). Pseudo-Athanasius presents Syncletica as teaching the following anthropological distinctions:

> There are three classes of opinions [*treis gnōmōn ideai*] about human life [*kata ton tōn anthrōpōn bion*] of which the first is [a life] of consummate evil [*tēs akrotatēs kakias*], and the second [a life] of a sort of middling state in that it looks out toward both while participating in one of the two, and the third, led toward greatness of contemplation [*eis megethos theōrias achtheisa*] not only holds herself together but also attempts to lead by hand those who are in the rear ranks. So the evil human beings, living among the inferior ones, all the more produce the increase of dreadful things, and the middling ones attempt to escape the undisciplined, fearing the same thing, lest again they be drawn down by them, for they are still like a child of the virtues, and the third, having vigorous minds and strong resolution, live together with and have converse with the common people, desiring to save them (Syncletica, *Life*, 71).

In this reversed hierarchy, from highest evil to the greatest contemplation, the monk categorizes humans ethically and by their influence on others:

the categories distinguish goodness/virtue, evil/vice, contemplation/dreadfulness, vigorous and weak minds, positive and negative effects on others. The vigorously minded and strongly willed contemplatives both provide for themselves and attempt to draw others with them from the middle, mixed category. The evil ones also attempt to drag the middle down with them. The ones in the middle are drawn from one to the other. All these beings are capable of activity and motion appropriate to the level of their ethical development.

Self-definition in relation to social groups:

In addition to the above categories of human being in relation to other beings, there are also classes of people in relation to whom the monk defines the self. The first distinction is between the "two classes" who were created to inhabit the earth: the married, whose function is to produce children, and the chaste, who were to live like angels. Both classes were called to holiness, but in different ways. This distinction is further refined when it defines the categories within chastity as the anchorites, the encratites, and those who live a moderate married life (See Clark, 1986a, 1986b; Pagels, 1985; Wicker). In an exegesis of the parable of the sower, Syncletica distinguishes three degrees of life: those who reap the hundredfold are those who live "our own profession" (*to hemeteron epaggelma*), which must be the monastic life; the sixtyfold are "the ranks of the self-controlled" (*to tōn egkratōn tagma*); the thirtyfold are "those who live with control over sensual desires" (*tōn sōphronōs biountōn*). She argues that it is better to progress from the control of desire to self-control, and then to the monastic life, and not in the reverse order (Syncletica, *Life*, 23).

The social body of the human being moves continually away from social entanglement and activity into solitude and quiet which becomes the ultimate goal of human existence. The progression moves from "married and physically engaged" to "married and chaste," then to "chaste and living with other chaste people," and ending with "chaste and solitary"; and it is valued as the progession from the lesser to the greater. Progress for humanity moves toward a non-social, solitary state:

> Just as the fetuses inside their womb, maturing from inferior food and life, are brought because of this to a greater security [*sōtēria*]; so also, the righteous withdraw from the ways of the world for the higher journey (Syncletica, *Life*, 91).

This withdrawal recalls the steady life of the angels in the earlier narrative about the fall and movement.

In marked contrast to our modern experience of body as bounded and limited, this monastic conception of a human being's social body is noticeably unbounded and fluid. Rising and falling between angels and daemons, and moving alternately toward the various polarities of virtues and vices, contemplation and licentiousness, social and sexual engagement and solitude, a human being has no fixed central point, no predetermined limits. The immovable boundaries of angels and daemons not only highlight the extremely movable and tenuous life of humans who struggle in both virtuous and contemplative arenas, they also provide a vast and fluid environment in which human beings are to function.

From within these various social distinctions (angel/human/daemon, good/mixed/evil, chaste/married), the monk emerges as a still more precise refinement. The monastic human being lives the angelic life on earth. This is a commonplace in monastic literature. Maximus the Confessor writes: "He that loves God leads an angelic life on earth, fasting and keeping watches, singing the psalter and praying, and always thinking good of everyone" (First Century, I.42). John Climacus' famous definition states: "Monasticism is an angelic order and state achieved in an earthly and soiled body" (Step I. 4, Moore #4, p. 4). The monk functions as an embodied angel who must through asceticism struggle not to fall, not to be dragged into evil, not to be lured into licentiousness. Conversely the monk, by developing in virtue, training the mind in contemplation, and rising each time there is a fall, lives the life of an angel on earth. The monk does not leave the fluid human state, nor does the monk find respite from activity and movement, but rather the angelic life as a goal gives direction and meaning to the ascetical struggle. The social body of the human being finds its highest aspiration in the life of an angel, a monk, who lives alone, having withdrawn more and more from the lower strata of social relations and being more and more oriented toward those above.

The Material Body of the Monk

The two social self-definitions of the monk lead directly to questions regarding the monk's view of the material body. Classic monastic anthropology understands the body as the arena for struggle. Although the daemons suggest that mortification of the flesh simply weakens it and wears it out unnecessarily, the strong monk recognizes that true spiritual strength and holiness are to be found in the punishment of the body. For example, Climacus writes:

> Let no one, when he is young, listen to his enemies, the demons, when they say to him: 'Do not wear out your flesh, lest you make it sick and weak.' For you will scarcely find anyone, especially in the present generation, who is determined to mortify his flesh, although he might deprive himself of many pleasant dishes. The aim of this demon is to make our very entrance into the stadium lax and negligent, and then make the end correspond to the beginning (*Ladder*, Step I, PG 641; Moore, #24, p. 10).

And Syncletica teaches:

> For neither is the devil [*diabolos*] prohibited by his first evil; but rather he also suggests change to the soul. And he subscribes that our ruling mind (is) a flower of nature, and that as the body is dissolved, even the soul will be destroyed. All these things he suggests to us so that the soul might be destroyed through negligence (*Life*, 88).

The monastic body, thus has become the athletic stadium for training toward victory through asceticism.

Since the body is an ascetical environment, the monk does not despise the body: it is too important a part of the monk's asceticism. Syncletica teaches that the gradual weakening of the body is advantageous:

> Let us not be distressed that because of the weakness and the striking of the body we are not able to stand for prayer or to sing with our voices: all these things are completed for the destruction of desires. For both fasting and sleeping on the ground have been made a law for us because of our most base pleasures. So if sickness has dulled them, the labor is redundant. Why do I say redundant? For just as by some greater and stronger drug, the death-dealing symptoms are put to rest by the sickness. And this is the great ascesis: to persevere in sicknesses and to send up thanksgiving hymns to the stronger. Have we been deprived of our eyes? Let us not suffer with disgust, for we have lost the organs of insatiate desire, but with the interior eyes we reflect the glory of the Lord. Have we become deaf? Let us give thanks that we have completely lost the vain hearing. Have we suffered with our hands? But we have the interior ones to prepare for the battle against the enemy. Does sickness totally conquer the body? But the health of the interior person will increase more (*Life*, 99).

Here it does not matter whether passive sickness or active ascetic practice diminishes the body because the effect is the same. The body contains desires which are to be destroyed; the body enjoys pleasures which must be quieted; the body has eyes and ears and other sense organs which must be oriented toward God alone. As a result the monk's body, thus sanctified by ascetic practice or sickness, becomes a healing agent to other monks: Syncletica's wounded body cured her disciples (Syncletica, *Life*, 110 and 107; see Brown, 1981).

Syncletica's body was, by virtue of her extreme illness, made the arena of her struggle. She suffered horrible sicknesses (*Life*, 106–113) which competely consumed her: she seems to have had lung cancer which eventually spread to her mouth. Her death, however, is not characterized as victory over the sick and decaying body, but as transformation, perfection, *in* the body:

> So, for three months she contended [*enathleō*] against this trial [*agōn*]. With divine power her whole body was supported [*parakrateō*], for the things which contributed toward its continuance had been diminished. Therefore, starvation [*atrophia*] was present, for how was she able to partake of victuals

while such putrefaction and stench prevailed? Even sleep, being smitten by her sufferings, withdrew from her. When the boundary of her victory and her crown was near, she beheld visions and attendants of angels [*aggelōn epistasias*], and (hosts of) holy virgins encouraging her ascension [*anodon*] and (she beheld) illuminations of ineffable light and the place of paradise. And after the spectacle of these things, as if it happened for herself, she announced to those arriving that they should bear themselves nobly and not belittle the present time (*Life*, 112–113).

The present, the time in her body, witnessed her transformation into an angelic being. In her body, with its now spiritualized sense organs and its dispassion toward food and sleep, she became that for which she had striven through asceticism. The passions at rest, she is without nourishment or sleep, and made capable of living the angelic life.

The monk simultaneously experiences the body as friend, ascetic arena, instrument of glorification, vessel of nature; and as foe, tyrant, and object for mastery (Harpham: 19–44). Climacus, at the very center of his ascetical scheme, portrays the monk as addressing his body:

> What is this mystery in me? What is the meaning of this blending [*synkrasis*] of body and soul? How am I constituted as a friend and foe to myself? Tell me, tell me, my yoke-fellow, my nature [*physis*], for I shall not ask anyone else in order to learn about you. How am I to remain unwounded by you? How can I avoid the danger of my nature? For I have already made a vow to Christ to wage war against you. How am I to overcome your tyrany? For I am resolved to be your master" (*Ladder*, Step XV, PG 904A-B; Moore, #89, p. 120).

The body is highly problematized, not simply rejected. The flesh, in turn, responds to the monk:

> And the flesh might say in reply to its soul: 'I shall never tell you anything which you do not know equally well, but only of things of which we both have knowledge [*gnōsis*]. I have my father within me—self-love. The fire which I experience from without comes from humouring me and from general comfort. The fire which burns within and the movement of thoughts come from past ease and bygone deeds. Having conceived, I give birth to sins; and they, when born, in turn beget death by despair. If you clearly know the profound weakness which is both you and me, you have bound my hands. If you starve your appetite, you have bound my feet from going further. If you take the yoke of obedience, you have thrown off my yoke. If you obtain humility, you have cut off my head' (*Ladder*, Step XV, PG 904A-B; Moore, #90, p. 120).

The body, conceiving through outward comfort and interior thoughts, produces sin which in turn begets despair and causes death. The bodily response to the bodily conception of sin and death is physical fasting and mental obedience. The body remains the origin of the human problem, the means to its remedy, and the environment of its final victory.

The physical body contains within itself the stimulus both to sin and to ascetical correction. For the monk, the daemons must be connected intimately to the body, and this connection is developed and preserved as part of the esoteric tradition of monastic asceticism. In a recent article , I argued that there was speculation regarding the ascetical significance of the formation of the body observable in the various formations of Adam's body in *The Apocryphon of John* and in the discussion of "is the soul the blood" in Origen's *Dialogue with Heraclides* (Valantasis, 1989). I further argued that Origen was in the process of making explicit the esoteric key to this knowledge. I maintain that such speculation on the ascetical significance of the formation of the material body continued to be a part of the monastic ascetic teaching and that it continued to be taught not as part of the *praktika*, but as part of the *gnostica* of monastic instruction (Cf. Dechow:297–347). Evidence for such a continued speculation is found in Evagrius Ponticus' *Ad Melaniam* as well as in his *Gnosticus* and his *Kephalaia Gnostica* (cf. Clark, 1990; O'Laughlin). Subsequent monastic texts, under the pressure of the Origenist condemnation or out of a tradition of keeping secret such gnostic speculations, have supressed the teaching on bodily formation and transformation, while at the same time keeping and continuing to teach the connection between bodily manipulation and the development of ascetical virtue. The clearest (and most straightforward) presentation of this speculation on the creation of the body comes from the earliest example in the *Apocryphon of John*, which I will use here to explore the systems underlying the monk's understanding of the body.

In the *Apocryphon of John*, three bodies are created: the first is the spiritual body of Adamas; the second is the primordial Adam created by the daemons and angels who must trick Ialdabaoth into breathing life into the inert body; the third is the purely material body created as a parody by the jealous powers.[5] The creation of three bodies (one spiritual, one psychic and one hylic) reflects an interest in clearly distinguishing hierarchies of being from the spiritual to the physical. However, if we avoid judgment on such categorization of bodies, we find interesting descriptions of the method of creation of each body. The creation of the "natural body" bears the greatest signification in relation to conceptual systems which may underlie the monastic tradition of the formation of the monastic body:

> This is the number of the angels: together they are 365. They all worked on it until, limb for limb, the natural and the material body was completed by them. Now there are other ones in charge over the remaining passions whom I did not mention to you. But if you wish to know them, it is written in the book of Zoroaster. And all the angels and demons worked until they had constructed the natural body. And their product was completely inactive and motionless for a long time (*Ap. John* 19:2–14).

The daemons and the angels create the natural body of which the passions are a part, and they rule over the passions. Such an understanding complements the monastic view of the body in which the body, as an athletic arena, is the environment for the control of the passions and desires as well as the arena for living the angelic life. The connection between vices, passions, and daemons in *The Apocryphon of John* further resonates with the monastic description of bodily asceticism, ethical development, and daemonic warfare:

> The four chief demons are: Ephememphi who belongs to pleasure, Yoko who belongs to desire, Nenentophni who belongs to grief, Blaomen who belongs to fear. And the mother of them all is Aesthesis-Ouch-Epi-Ptoe. And from the four demons passions came forth. And from grief (came) envy, jealousy, distress, trouble, pain, callousness, anxiety, mourning, etc. And from pleasure much wickedness arises, and empty pride, and similar things. And from desire (comes) anger, wrath, and bitterness, and bitter passion, and unsatedness, and similar things. And from fear (comes) dread, fawning, agony, and shame. All of these are like useful things as well as evil things. But the insight into their true character is Anaro, who is the head of the material soul, for it belongs with the seven senses, Ouch-Epi-Ptoe (*Ap. John* 18:2–19:1; See also Syncletica, *Life*, 85 and 96).

The body was a complex society inhabited by daemons and angels and whose parts were ruled by them. The four chief passions (pleasure, desire, grief, and fear), which the four named chief daemons manifest, are not by nature evil; they are neutral elements indigenous to bodily existence. The passions naturally form a part of the body, so living with the passions requires careful observation and a diagnostics of the body, as Climacus explains:

> As bodily fever is one thing, but the causes of this are not one but many, so also the boiling up of anger and the movement of our other passions have many and various causes. That is why it is impossible to prescribe one identical rule for them. Instead, I would rather suggest that each of those who are sick should most carefully seek out his own particular cure. The first step in the cure should be the diagnosis of the cause of each disease; for when this is discovered, the patients will get the right cure from God's care and from their spiritual physicians. And so, for instance, those who wish to join us in the Lord should enter the spiritual tribunal that lies before us, and there they should test themselves somewhat concerning the abovementioned passions or their causes (*Ladder*, Step VIII, PG 833C-D; Moore, #29, pp. 85–86).

The same kinds of passions which the *Apocryphon of John* describe as neutral are described by the monks as negative. The monk must discern and confront the passions in order to master them: the monk must capture each passion through vigilance, fasting, mental prayer and thereby gain mastery over them through knowledge.

This mastery over the body and its passions, the hallmark of achieving the angelic and solitary life, results from rendering the body as a corpse, or, in other words, from the "mortification" of the body. The monk's body, already experienced as a community of angelic and daemonic elements in conflict, must be so stilled that it is, for every purpose, dead. Syncletica teaches this in its most stark reality:

> For our profession [*epaggelma*] is nothing other than the renunciation of life [*apotagē biou*], the practice of death [*meletē thanatou*]. Therefore just as the dead do not operate in the body, so neither do we (*Life*, 76).

Even though the renunciation of life constitutes the mortification of the body, the body nonetheless manifests the angelic life. Climacus describes the embodied life of the monk in this way:

> At the gate of your heart place strict and unsleeping guards. Restrain your unrestrainable mind within your active body. Amidst the actions and movements of your limbs, practice noetic stillness [*hesychia*]. And most paradoxical of all, in the midst of commotion, be unmoved in soul. Curb your tongue which rages to leap into arguments. Seventy times seven in the day wrestle with this tyrant. Fix your mind to your soul as to the wood of the cross, to be struck like an anvil with blow upon blow of the hammers, to be mocked, abused, ridiculed and wronged, without being in the least crushed or broken, but continuing to be quite calm and immovable (*Ladder*, Step IV, PG 700B-D, Moore # 36, p. 35).

The angelic life, manifested in the body, emerges from the control of the body and of bodily movements.

The monk's mind (*nous*) plays such a major part that it has become the most critical human faculty. The mind, as in Climacus' description above, may remain still when the body is active. Conversely, the mind may remain active when the body is still. Climacus explains that the mind continues to wage the war against the daemons even when the body is at rest:

> When we are lying in bed, let us be especially sober and vigilant, because then our mind without our body struggles with the demons, and if it [sc. the mind] is found to be fond of delight [*philēdonos*], it readily becomes a traitor (*Ladder*, PG 889C-D, Step XV, Moore [slightly altered] # 53, p. 112).

The mind re-orients the monk from a concern with the body and its passions to the things of the soul: the mind, under the influence of prayer, turns the monk's attention toward God. The mind divinizes the monk's body. Maximus explains the process:

> Thoughts are directed to things. Now, of things some are sense-perceptible, some mental. The mind, then, tarrying with these things, carries about with itself thoughts of them; but the grace of prayer joins the mind to God, and joining to God withdraws it from every thought. Then the mind, associating only with Him, becomes God-like (*Ascetic Life*, #24, p.116).

The monk's body engages in a complex process of control: the body contains within itself the daemonic and the angelic elements which rule it, so the body must be mortified. The process of mortification relies upon the distinction, minimally, between the sense-perceptible and the mental. The mind subdues the body in prayer and ascetical activity, and begins to be rid of the images and thoughts which turn the monk away from God. The mind, through further prayer, becomes oriented toward God and becomes God-like in the bodily state. The monk's progress both begins and ends in the body: in the beginning the body consists of the society of daemons, angels, and body parts; in the end, the body is subdued, still, and solitary in its union with God.

This conceptual model of the monk's body makes the body a living metaphor of the desert: the monastic body, withdrawn from social life, far from social engagement and politics has become a desert, a solitary body, punished by the environment. Like the desert the body is even inhabited by daemons.

Part Two: Monastic Daemonology

Although the daemons function within the sphere of the monk's corporeal and social body, they are discussed as though they were purely exterior forces whose impact was experienced interiorly. In fact, the daemons are the only constant companion for a monk who has withdrawn from the world. Monastic daemonology will be explored under three categories: the daemon's characteristics; the daemon's manner of interaction with the monks; and the methods in daemonic warfare.

The Daemon's Characteristics

John Climacus described the daemons as "strong; they never sleep; they are incorporeal and invisible" (*Ladder*, Step I, PG 641, Moore, #24, pp. 9–10). Daemons are lighter than the human body, being capable of flying suspended in the air. Their ability to float enables them to see what is about to happen before humans can see it; they appear, therefore, to be able to predict the future, even though this is simply the result of their lighter bodily construction (*Ladder*, Step IV, PG 672, Moore # 28, pp. 19–20).

Daemons are "spirits" (*pneumata* [*Ladder*, Step IV; PG 712A-B; Moore, #69, p. 42]) who rule everywhere except in heaven. Climacus relates the following daemonic self-revelation:

> At last, when flogged, they said: 'We have neither beginning nor birth, for we are progenitors and parents of all the passions. Contrition of heart that is

born of obedience is our real enemy; we cannot bear to be subject to anyone; that is why we fell from Heaven, though we had authority there. In brief, we are the parents of all that opposes humility; for everything which furthers humility, opposes us. We hold sway everywhere, save in heaven, so where will you run from our presence? We often accompany dishonours, and obedience, and freedom from anger, and lack of resentment, and service. Our offspring are the falls of spiritual men: anger, calumny, spite, irritability, shouting, blasphemy, hypocrisy, hatred, envy, disputation, self-will and disobedience. There is only one thing in which we have no power to meddle; and we shall tell you this, for we cannot bear your blows: If you keep up a sincere condemnation of yourself before the Lord, you can count us as weak as a cobweb. For pride's saddle-horse, as you see, is vainglory, on which I am mounted' (*Ladder*, Step XXIII, PG 896C-D, Moore, #37, pp. 141–42).

The daemons reveal that they are without beginning or origin (*archē*) and without birth (*gennesis*). Their unbegotten and unoriginate state has enabled them to be the "progenitors and parents of all the passions." The daemons, still in this confession, state that they fell from heaven where they had authority, so they cannot bear to be subject to anyone. Pride, therefore, is their chief weapon. Daemons are prevalent: they function everywhere and no one can hide from them. Their children are the vices which cause spiritual people to fall: "anger, calumny, spite, irritability, shouting, blasphemy, hypocrisy, hatred, envy, disputation, self-will and disobedience." Only when the monk acquires the virtue of humility can they be defeated.

Climacus' description echoes the description of the relationship of daemons to passion in *The Apocryphon of John* (18:2–19:1). The daemons, themselves unoriginate yet fallen, have conceived all the evil passions, and those passions, woven into the monk's body, have become the community in which the monk will grow into humility.[6] Such a community presents no easy way; some monks even expressed a preference for the easier contest with the brethren in the community than for the daemonic warfare of more spiritual powers precisely because it was a more difficult warfare with a more formidable set of opponents. John Climacus explains:

> I must not fail to adorn the crown of this step with this emerald. Once I started a discussion on stillness with some of the most experienced elders in the community. With a smile on their faces and in jovial mood, they said to me in a friendly way: 'We, Father John, being material, live a material life, preferring to wage war according to the measure of our weakness, and considering it better to struggle with men, who are sometimes fierce and sometimes repentant, than with the demons who are continually raging and up in arms against us' (*Ladder*, Step IV, PG 700B; Moore, Step 4, #35, p. 35).

The daemons, then, in their ruling everywhere except in heaven, rule also in the monk's body. It is their character to incite the passions and thereby to set the stage for the monk's progress: the daemons employ their cunning specifically to entrap or preclude the monk's successful combat with the particular passions which present that monk with the greatest difficulty. In this capacity, the daemons determine the form and content of ascetical activity. The daemons preserve their rule, while the monk, in order to encourage ascetical activity, characterizes the daemons as "other," "foe," "the enemy," "the adversaries."

The monks describe the daemons as an invisible army. For the monks the daemons are highly organized, hierarchical, and combative forces whose primary purpose is to destroy the monk's virtue. Climacus explains:

> We ought to consider whether our spiritual enemies have not each their own proper task to fulfil when drawn up in battle array against us, just as in a visible war. Suprising to say, they certainly have. When I thought about those who were tempted, I observed that falls were of varying seriousness. He that hath ears to hear, let him hear (*Ladder*, XV, PG 885A; Moore XV, #28, p. 107).

From the monk's perspective, the daemons wage a well-conceived battle by attacking in ways the monk would least expect:

> The devil often has the habit, especially in warring against ascetics and those leading the solitary life, of using all his force, all his zeal, all his cunning, all his intrigue, all his ingenuity and purpose, to assail them by means of what is unnatural, and not by what is natural. Therefore, ascetics coming into contact with women, and not in any way tempted either by desire or thought, have sometimes regarded themselves as already blessed, not knowing, poor things, that where a worse downfall had been prepared for them, there was no need of the lesser one (*Ladder*, Step XV, PG 885B; Moore #29, pp. 107–108).

In warfare, the daemons systematically undermine the monks' ability to live dispassionately and quietly by creating for them a false dispassion and quiet.

The fact, however, that daemons and monks are locked in such intimate conflict and mutual knowledge confirms that their relationship is primary. Those monks who live in community do battle primarily with other members of the community: their battle field develops in the natural course of trying to become "perfect" in the context of community living. The hesychast who represents the higher form of life, the life toward which the monks aspire, battles the daemons. The communal life, explored as a secondary level of monastic life, prepares the monk for the "higher" life of the solitary hesychast. The monastic life progresses then from community living to solitary life, from fellowship with brothers and sisters to the constant companionship of the daemons:

> Those living in stillness [*hesychia*] subject to a father have only demons working against them. But those living in a community struggle with demons and human beings. The former, being always under the eyes of the master, keep his commands more strictly; but the latter, on account of his absence, break

them to some extent. However, those who are zealous and industrious more than make up for this failing by enduring collisions and knocks, and win double crowns (*Ladder*, Step IV, PG 712C; Moore, #76, p. 43).

Their mutual companionship cannot always be characterized as antagonistic. The monks do not understand daemons to be "evil" or "evil forces" which the monks must reject. The monk's companionship with the daemons is one of growth-oriented antagonism. Consider this description of a conversation:

> One who had the gift of sight told me what he had seen. 'Once,' he said, 'when I was sitting in an assembly, the demon of vainglory and the demon of pride came and sat beside me, one on either side. The one poked me in the side with the finger of vainglory and urged me to relate some vision of labour which I had done in the desert. But as soon as I had shaken him off, saying: Let them be turned back and confounded that desire evils for me [Ps 39:20], then the demon on my left at once said in my ear: Well done, well done, you have become great by conquering my shameless mother. Turning to him, I made apt use of the rest of the verse and said: Let them be turned back straightway in shame that say unto me: Well done! well done!' And to my question: 'How is vainglory the mother of pride?' he replied: 'Praises exalt and puff one up; and when the soul is exalted, then pride seizes it, lifts it up to heaven and casts it down to the abyss' (*Ladder*, Step XXII, PG 953C-D; Moore, #35, p. 136).

This conversation highlights the nature and import of the relationship: the daemons constantly interact with the monk in order to force the monk's spiritual growth. Without the presence of the monk's striving, the daemons would be perceived as friendly: it is precisely the monk's striving that constructs the daemons negatively. Since the monks have left their normal habitat to live in the natural habitat of the daemons, the conflict between monks and daemons has as much to do with the conflict between natural geographical spheres of influence as with the presence of mutually adversarial companions:

> As we have said before, some people in hermitages suffer far more severe attacks from the enemy. And no wonder! For the demons haunt such places, since the Lord in His care for our salvation has driven them into the deserts and the abyss. Demons of fornication cruelly assail the hesychast in order to drive him back into the world, as having received no benefit from the desert. Demons keep away from us when we are living in the world, that we may go on staying among worldly-minded people because we are not attacked there. Hence we should realize that the place in which we are attacked is the one in which we are certainly waging bitter war on the enemy; for if we ourselves are not waging war, the enemy is found to be our friend (*Ladder*, Step XV, PG 893A-B; Moore, #62, pp. 113–114).

This relationship does not describe a confrontation between good and evil (to any degree) but rather a kind of circumstantial adversarial companionship. The circumstances revolve about the natural geographical spheres of habitation, the body's natural relationship with its parts, and the monk's desire to transform the body into some sort of angelic body. Ironically, the monk lives in the daemons' world in order to get free of the body (which the daemons have helped to create): the monk's goal is to live as a corpse, or as an angel, both of which seem to result in the same transformation. The daemons, already bodiless, hover over the monk in order to restrain the monk's transformation and to maintain control both over the monk's body and the geographical terrain in which they rule.

The Daemons' Interaction with the Monks

These descriptions of the daemons as simultaneously friend and enemy, natural companion and supernatural enemy, lead directly to the discussion of the nature of the interaction between monks and daemons. The ambiguous companionship of monk and daemon provides the context for their equally peculiar manner of relation. The daemons strive to thwart the monk's ascetical transformation (see, for example, Climacus, *Ladder*, Step VII, PG 816C; Moore, #68, p. 80) through both exterior bodily and interior mental attacks:

> It is necessary, therefore, always to be vigilant [*grēgorein*]. For he fights through external matters and subdues through internal thoughts [*logismōn*]. And he does much more through the internal, for by night and in the course of the day he draws near immaterially (Syncletica, *Life*, 28).

The daemons do not attack directly, but prefer to overcome monks because they are found to be negligent or because they (experiencing an increment of success) have been discovered to be arrogant:

> A twofold fear is placed on you: either [a fear] lest you return to the former things through negligence when the enemy attacks you; or (a fear) lest you shall be tripped while running. For our enemy the devil [*diabolos*] either draws one to himself from behind at whatever time he sees that the soul is slow and sluggish, or, when it seems to be excellent and patient of toil toward ascesis, he enters afterward subtly and covertly by means of arrogance, and in this way, he destroys the soul together with the person (Syncletica, *Life*, 49).

The daemons' attacks, moreover, consistently move from interior to exterior, from one set of vices to another, shifting the arena of the monks' attention and practice:

> And what were his first traps? Clearly [they were] gluttony, love of pleasures, fornication. These spirits especially happen at the more youthful ages. Greed, covetousness and things like them follow after these. So the struggling soul, when it survives these passions, supposing that it might rule the stomach, when also it might leap over the pleasures of the belly with dignity, when it might despise money, then, from all quarters the malicious one,

perplexed, subjects undisciplined movement upon the soul (Syncletica, *Life*, 49).

Since the daemons set traps for ensnaring monks, the monks must constantly remain vigilant. This cycle of entrapment and vigilence defines the primary manner of their relating.

The monks' vigilance, consequently, must become increasingly more sophisticated with ascetical progress because the daemons customize their assault to the weakness of each individual monk:

> The adversary [*ho enantios*] sets this rationale before those who turn from worldly wisdom to the solitary life, for the devil [*diabolos*] who is sensible about evil things places traps for human nature. To some he persists through [their] despair, and he draws some down through vanity, and he buries others because of their love of money. For, like a death-dealing doctor, he brings poisons to humans. And one person he destroys through the liver, bringing him the toxin of desire; another he makes wounded in the heart, fastening his temper to anger; and he dulls the authoritative power of some, either wrapping them with ignorance, or twisting them through useless learning (Syncletica, *Life*, 85).

Each of these vices evolves from the three primary daemonic origins of all vices: the first is bodily pleasure, the second is psychic desire, and the third is a grief which mixes both bodily and psychic elements. These principal monastic faults, which reflect the listing in *Ap. John* 18:2–19:1, define for the daemons the principal areas of monastic weakness while providing for the monks the foundational areas for vigilance of body and psyche:

> There are three principal heads of the enemy, from which all evil descends: desire, pleasure, grief. These depend one upon the other, and one follows from the other: it is possible moderately to rule over pleasure, but it is impossible [to rule over] desire. For the former (that is, the one) regarding pleasure is accomplished through the body, but the latter arises from the soul. But grief is constructed from both of them. So do not allow desire to function and you will disperse the remaining things (Syncletica, *Life*, 96).

The monks' vigilance focuses on desire, while the daemons may attack from a wide spectrum of the passions derivative from desire.

Practicing a sort of impish delight in trapping monks, daemons employ a variety of techniques. The daemons use the monks' memory to remind them of family and to suggest their families' grief at their withdrawal:

> After our renunciation, when the demons inflame our hearts by reminding us of our parents and brethren, then let us arm ourselves against them with prayer, and let us inflame ourselves with the remembrance of the eternal fire, so that by reminding ourselves of this, we may quench the untimely fire of our heart. If anyone thinks he is without attachment to some object, but is

grieved at its loss, then he is completely deceiving himself (Climacus, *Ladder*, Step II, PG, 657; Moore, #10 and 11, pp.13-14).

Or they may transform themselves into angels or martyrs and suggest that the monk is in communion with them:

> Demons often transform themselves into angels of light and take the form of martyrs, and make it appear to us during sleep that we are in communication with them. Then, when we wake up, they plunge us into unholy joy and conceit. But you can detect their deceit by this very fact. For angels reveal torments, judgments and separations; and when we wake up we find that we are trembling and sad. As soon as we begin to believe the demons in dreams, then they make sport of us when we are awake too. He who believes in dreams is completely inexperienced. But he who distrusts all dreams is a wise man. Only believe dreams that warn you of torments and judgments. But if despair afflicts you, then such dreams are also from the demons (Climacus, *Ladder*, Step IV, PG 672A-B; Moore, #29, p. 20).

The daemons may also depart from the monk to deceive the monk into thinking that the warfare has ended:

> And we ought not to forget, my friends, that the wicked demons sometimes suddenly leave us, so that we may neglect our strong passions as of little importance, and then become incurably sick (*Ladder*, Step VIII, PG, 829A; Moore #9, p. 82; see also Step XXVI, PG 1025C; Moore #61, p. 170).

Or contrarily, the daemons may suggest as warfare the very ascetical practice which will increase the monk's most problematic passion and lead to a fall:

> If we are observant, we shall see that many irritable people are practising vigils, fasts and stillness. For the aim of the demons is to suggest to them, under the pretext of repentance and mourning, just what is likely to increase their passion (*Ladder*, Step VIII, PG 832C-D; Moore, #21, p. 84).

The daemons push the monk to sin, and when the monk cannot be provoked to the intended sin, the daemons then lead the monk to another sin—judgment of others who have sinned:

> The demons, murderers as they are, push us into sin. Or if they fail to do this, they get us to pass judgment on those who are sinning, so that they may defile us with the stain which we ourselves are condemning in another (*Ladder* X, PG 848C; Moore, #11, p. 91).

Finally, the daemons suggest means for the monk to experiment carefully with sins while using either the memory of sinful acts to defeat the monk or the monk's ignorance of sin to encourage sinful experimentation:

> The snake of sensuality is many-faced. In those who are inexperienced in sin, he sows the thought of making one trial and then stopping. But this crafty creature incites those who have tried this to fresh trial through the remem-

brance of their sin. Many inexperienced people feel no conflict in themselves simply because they do not know what is bad; and the experienced, because they know this abomination, suffer disquiet and struggle. But often the opposite of this also happens (*Ladder*, Step XV, PG 896A; Moore, #68, p. 115).

Each of these daemonic methods relies upon an appearance of propriety and an inversion of expectation and reality:

During temptation, I have felt that this wolf was producing incomprehensible joy, tears and consolation in my soul, but I was really being deceived, when I so childishly thought to have fruit from this and not harm (*Ladder*, Step XV, PG888 D; Moore, #42, p. 110).

The daemons entrap the monk, using every means to keep the monk linked to the passions:

Let us watch and see (for perhaps in season, we may void gall by bitterness) which of the demons uplift us, which cast us down, which harden, which comfort, which darken, which pretend to communicate enlightenment to us, which make us slothful, which make us cunning, which make us sad, and which cheerful (*Ladder*, Step XXVI, PG 1073C: Moore, #184, p. 191).

With such constant and ever-changing daemonic possibilities, the monks must constantly and consistently be aware of themselves and vigilant against further surprising attacks.

The daemons' companionship with the monk provides them with information about the monk's weakness while at the same time developing the monk's ability to discern the tricks of the adversary. The monk gains self-mastery and self-knowledge because the daemons provide constant and ever more subtle opportunities for self-examination, self-control, and self-understanding. Without the daemons, the monks would not be able to advance or to achieve their goals. The more subtle the daemonic attack, the greater the monks' achievement.

Methods in Daemonic Warfare

Five methods are discernible in the descriptions by monks of their warfare with the daemons. I have organized these methods to move from the most concrete and embodied concerns to the more etherial.

In the first method, the daemons attempt to preserve the monks' social body as a socially engaged body. In this initial phase of the monastic life, the monks' memories of family are enflamed by the daemons during waking hours (Climacus, *Ladder*, Step II, PG 657, Moore #10 and 11, pp. 13–14), and during sleep the daemons "try to disturb us with dreams, representing to us that our relatives are either grieving or dying, or are held captive for our sake and are destitute" (*Ladder*, Step IV, PG 669B-C; Moore #27, p. 19). The monastic life cannot be lived without a withdrawal both from the social body and from the physical, so the monks initially attack the social body, rendering the physical incapacitated in the next method.

In the second method of warfare the daemons attack the monks' physical body:

> The daemon battles with those in obedience, sometimes to defile them with bodily pollutions, and make them hard-hearted, and sometimes to make them more agitated than usual. At other times, he makes them dry and barren, sluggish in prayer, drowsy and benighted, in order to tear them away from their struggle by making them think they have gained nothing by their obedience, but are only backsliding. For he does not allow them time to reflect that often the providential withdrawal of our imagined goods or blessings leads us to the deepest humility (*Ladder*, Step IV, PG 708B; Moore, #58, p.40).

The daemons attempt to thwart the monks' mental prayer and concentration which are the means of achieving mastery over the daemons, "[f]or by distractions, the daemons aim to bring our prayer to nothing" (*Ladder*, Step IV, PG 717A; Moore, #101, p. 46; see also Step V, PG 777C-D; Moore, #29–30, p. 64; and in relation to accedie, Step XIII; PG 860B-C; Moore #8, p. 96). It is only through mental activity and prayer that the monk is capable of mastering the body and the daemons: "Be concentrated [*synnous*] without self-display, withdrawn into your heart. For the demons fear concentration as thieves fear dogs" (*Ladder*, Step VII, PG 805A; Moore, #15, p. 72). The pure body of the monk makes God rejoice and the defiled monastic body makes the daemons rejoice:

> The Lord, being incorruptible and incorporeal, rejoices in the purity and incorruptibility of our body. But nothing gives such joy to the demons, some say, as the stench [*dysōdia*] of fornication; and no other passion so gladdens them as the defilement of the body (*Ladder*, Step XV, PG 888B; Moore, #35, p. 109).

These attacks on the monk's body intend to force the monk back into society, into marriage, sexual relations, familial responsibility. The first two methods mirror one another.

In the third method of warfare, daemons wage mental warfare. The daemons attempt to weaken the monk's mind using a number of techniques. First, they attack using the memory so that the remembrance of sin might discourage the monk and lead to a fall (*Ladder*, Step XV, PG 896A; Moore, #68, p. 115). Next they will "darken the mind" of the monk "and then they will suggest whatever they like" (*Ladder*, Step XV, PG 901A; Moore, #81, p. 119). The daemons fill the minds of the inexperienced with impossible goals and those of the experienced with images of hospitality and ministry that will distract them from their immediate pursuit (*Ladder*, Step IV, PG 725B; Moore, #118, p. 52). In Climacus there is even a tabulation of a new mental trick called the "flick of the mind" (*pararrhipismon noos*) which particularly distresses the monk:

> Amongst the more precise and discerning Fathers, there is mention of a still more subtle notion, something which some of them call a flick of the mind [*pararrhipismon noos*]. This is its characteristic: without passage of time, without word or image, it instantaneously introduces the passion to the victim. There is nothing swifter or more indiscernible among spirits. It manifests itself in the soul by a simple remembrance, which is instantaneous, independent, inapprehensible, and, in some cases, even unknown to the person himself. If anyone, therefore, with the help of mourning has been able to detect such a subtlety, he can explain to us how it is possible for a soul, by the eye alone, by a mere glance, or the touch of the hand, or the hearing of a song, without any notion or thought, to commit a definite sin of impurity (*Ladder*, Step XV, PG 897B-C; Moore #75, pp. 116–17).

By manipulating the monk's mind, the daemons disable the monk's ability both to understand and to resist the daemonic warfare.

Method four is related to the mental warfare: it is the presentation to the monks of fantasies that they have achieved a high status (see Climacus, *Ladder*, Step IV, PG 708B-C, Moore, #59, p. 40) and that they no longer need to be concerned about their spiritual progress (Step XV, PG 885 B; Moore #29, pp. 107–8). These fantasies appeal directly to the monks' arrogance and pride, and cause serious falls. The daemons even achieve this by withdrawing from the monk, bringing a temporary end to the warfare, which in turn creates the image that the monk has already arrived at perfection, or the angelic life, or the communion of angels and martyrs.

In the final, fifth method of warfare, the daemons become angels of light. They become what the monks most deeply desire to see and to be, so that the monks, believing that they have received visions and prophesies and that they are a part of the gloriously transformed angels on earth, are deceived and fall even further (see Climacus, *Ladder*, Step IV, PG 672A-B, Moore #29, p. 20). Toward the end of his *Ladder*, Climacus writes:

> When the demon of pride gets a foothold in his servants, he appears to them either in sleep or in a waking vision, as though in the form of a holy angel or some martyr, and gives them a revelation of mysteries, or a free bestowal of spiritual gifts, so that these unfortunates may be deceived and completely lose their wits (Step XXIII, PG 968C-D; Moore, #19, p. 140).

At this level, the monks remain vulnerable to the most deceptive of attacks, so their discernment and subtle understanding of themselves and of the daemons' work is crucial to their success.

Monastic daemonology, as it has been developed here, revolves about an intense relationship between monks and the daemons which rule over the monks' bodies and who also regulate the development of virtue for the monks through a constant process of testing. In this monastic daemonology monks and daemons are companions in the ascetic way.

Part Three: Monastic Asceticism

From the perspective of monastic anthropology and monastic daemonology, it is now possible to discuss monastic asceticism. Without the conception of the social body of the human being and the physical body of the monk, and without the creative role of daemons in the body's passions, monastic ascetic activity may be thought to have "produced some star ascetic athletes, whose achievements in devising ever more eccentric tortures for their own bodies might seem to have eclipsed all competition in body renunciation" (Williams, 1989:129). But once the monk's ascetical activity is located in the body (both social and material), and once the monk's development is understood to occur through the bodily control of bodily functions materialized as daemons, then monastic asceticism becomes significantly embodied and its goal that of experiencing in the body the most profound quiet and communion with God.

Monastic asceticism, then, is *not* other-worldly asceticism. The monk receives reward for ascetical labor in this world, in the body, in the society of monks and angels:

> You see how in loosing every band of wickedness from our hearts and in undoing every knot of contracts forced for grudges, and in hastening to do good for our neighbor with our whole soul—you see how we are illumined with the light of knowledge, and freed from the disgrace of passions, and filled with every virtue; and are illumined by God's glory and freed from every ignorance; and praying for things after Christ's mind, we are heard and shall have God with us continually and are filled with godly desire (Maximus, *Discourse*, #41, p. 133).

Monastics aim to become gods, to be deified (cf. Valantasis, 1990), by their ascetical labor:

> Therefore let us give ourselves entirely to the Lord, that we may receive Him again entire. Let us become gods through Him, for on that account He became man, who is by nature God and Master. Let us obey Him and He will without trouble vindicate us against our enemies (Maximus, Discourse, #43, p. 134).

This goal is consistent and expressed in various monastic literatures in remarkably similar language. The monk's body becomes divine by mastering the passions and the crafty daemons who rule them. This mastery perfects the body in virtue and brings the monk to an illuminating knowledge of God while transporting the monk into an immediate communion with God (cf. Valantasis, 1991:13–33). The goal of the monastic life, and the end of ascetical activity, is the perfecting of the monk's body.

Asceticism manages the perfecting of the monk's body. Asceticism, however, is a metaphor because it uses a concept taken from sports to explain a religious way of life. As a metaphor, asceticism explains the monk's experience through the experience of an athlete training for a contest: both the monk and the athlete must train, must carefully develop and regulate their bodily functions, must take into account the competition, and must pursue vigorously the victorious prize.

The metaphorical structure in monastic asceticism, however, is even more complex because "monastic asceticism" employs two other sophisticated metaphoric systems, viz. the "monk" and "daemons." The "monk" defines a complex social and religious re-location of the body and its relationship to angels and God by means of a particular social isolation and withdrawal. That is, the monk defines the transformation of body and its relationships which the monk experiences by talking about systems of withdrawal from society and body. Daemons are personifications of human experience used to explain the complex relationship between the parts of the body, the body's desires and activities, and the natural resistance to bodily change in the development of virtue. Each one of these systems (monastic anthropology, monastic daemonology, and monastic asceticism) are metaphorical because each explains some aspect of the monastic life by reference to another system of knowledge.

The literary study of metaphor, however, has treated metaphor primarily as rhetorical device and embellishment, and therefore has on the whole not seriously considered metaphor to be central to either culture or experience. And yet in monastic ascetical culture, metaphors creatively connect particular physical experience, general culture and understanding, and spiritual education.

The recent work of George Lakoff and Mark Johnson on metaphor develops a useful experientially based system of understanding of which metaphor is one element. They argue that the human body, the physical and cultural environment in which human beings live structures human experience.

> Recurrent experience leads to the formation of categories, which are experiential gestalts with those natural dimensions. Such gestalts define coherence in our experience ... [Direct human understanding occurs when human experience is perceived] directly from interaction with and in our environment.... We understand experience metaphorically when we use a gestalt from one domain of experience to structure experience in another domain (Lakoff and Johnson: 230).

Both asceticism and daemonology are metaphoric systems in which the metaphor organizes and communicates the experience of the monk: the activity of the daemon is a metaphor because it is a gestalt from one domain used to organize and explain the monastic experience.

The identification of these systems as metaphoric redirects our attention. The daemons, even in monastic literature, have been incorporated into a complex system of interrelated narratives: (1) about the Fall of human beings (either in Gnostic speculation or in Christian and Jewish exegesis of Genesis 1–3); or (2) about the warfare resulting from the fall of angels who become devils with an army of daemons; (3) about the fall of human beings through the sin of Adam and Eve and their expulsion from paradise which has necessitated a divine savior; or (4) about the identification of the Christian with the warfare reminiscent of Jesus' warfare with the devil in the desert as a form of the imitation of Christ. These narratives disguise the fact that the monastic ascetical systems really concern the monk's experience and perfection of the body through withdrawal, because these narratives each direct attention to the historical sequences (body in society, body out of society, body fighting daemons in the desert like Jesus, body victorious in resisting devil, body crowned with victory). In monastic asceticism, however, the primary motivation to fight daemons relates not to the imitation of Christ, or to the myth of redemption or rising from a fall, or any other narrative, but to the perfecting of the monk's body.

Monastic asceticism is *not* a personal appropriation and undoing of a Fall narrative, but the writing in life, in the world, in the body, of transformative practices aimed at perfecting and divinizing the body. The distinction between various types of asceticism may relate, then, not so much to the ascetical practices themselves, or to the physical manipulation of the body for the production of a divinized body, but rather to the narrative structures which give meaning to these practices by placing them within an interpretive frame. It is conceivable that the difference between the asceticism of certain Gnostic groups (termed by ecclesiastical authority as "heretical") and the asceticism of the monks (termed "orthodox") relates not to the understanding and working of the body, but to the narratives to which each assigns the significance of their ascetic practice. The narratives about daemonic warfare indicate whether or not the ascetical practices are considered dualistic. The emergent catholic church, for example, deemed the asceticism of the Sethian and Valentinian gnostics who developed a complex mythological structure and narrative, as "heretical;" and "gnostic" ascetics disparaged the lack of perception on the parts of "orthodox" practitioners. Both groups shared similar methods of asceticism, related conceptions of the formation of the body, correlative understandings of the relationship of corporeality to virtue, and practically identical formulations of the goal of ascetical activity. The monks aspire to the divinization of the body identified as the corpse, the hylic body. The various narratives about the formation and redemption of the body locate the body which is being perfected. For those ascetics (gnostic or monastic) who wished to preserve a strict delimitation between body and spirit in their narratives, this perfectible body was definitely not the hylic body which the jealous powers created, but the psychic and the pneumatic body which the daemons and angels constructed and into which the life-breath was breathed. For the monks discussed in this paper, however, all of these bodies are collapsed into one: the body from the Fall narrative, the angelic body, the hylic body meet in the monk, and it is that monk's body which will be divinized.

The monk's body by definition is a withdrawn body, a body removed from its normal social environment and placed in what is experienced as an hostile environment. Asceticism, then, must take into account the body (here including those body parts ruled by the daemons) and the environment in which that body must live. A series of (at least) four withdrawals or changes in environment perfects the monk's body: withdrawal from family and society; entrance into a community; withdrawal from community to a hermitage; living in the angelic body. Each withdrawal or change in environment creates an altered awareness of the body and its functions (both socially and physically). By controlling the body at each of these stages, the monk becomes knowledgeable about the body and the environment, acquiring more sophisticated knowledge about the complex interactions of social body, physical body, and environment.

The monk first withdraws from family and society to begin a strict regimen of fasting, sleep deprivation, and mental prayer. The monk gains mastery over the body's need for nourishment and rest, while at the same time being weaned from the body's need for pleasure and sexual enjoyment and from the person's need for companionship. The first two methods of daemonic warfare (the daemonic attack on the social and physical body of the monk) occur during this initial stage. The environment is defined primarily by where it is not: it is not a familiar setting, but foreign space.

The second stage is a withdrawal into community, or an entrance into monastic community. Here the close proximity of community forces the monk to become aware of the psycho-physical responses to incarceration, as well as the effect of the passions emergent from close living. The passions (particularly anger, and others that emerge from a loss of self-will and self-regulation) emerge as the center of the struggle. The monk must learn, by obedience and humility, to blend with the community. The monk's body must voluntarily become a member of another social body by controlling the will and the drive to control. In this stage the development of social virtues and the learning of mental prayer and concentration in the midst of community constitute the daemon's third stage of warfare.

In the next stage, the monk withdraws from the community to a hermitage, from companionship to the solitary life. The monk enters the most initmate relationship with the body, recognizing and mastering the most persistent of bodily reactions manifested as daemonic warfare. In this body the monk masters both the voluntary and the involuntary bodily functions, learning to still the body and to bring bodily activity to its most quiescent state. The daemons' attack concentrates on the creation of fantasies and images of perfection, so that the monk is deceived into thinking that this body is the final state. The subtle body-knowledge that emerges becomes increasingly sophisticated.

The final stage is the monk's body at rest, the angelic or divinized body. The monk must practice great discernment, because in the prior stage the daemons suggest this victory. But when it happens, it is evident and visible in the body. Anthony the Great, Syncletica, the great monks of the desert tradition, all experienced this final victory. The monk's body, stilled, unmoved, dried out, unaffected by passion, turns all of its sensual and physical attention toward God.

The function of the daemons in each of these stages remains the same. Daemons expose both the voluntary and involuntary, natural and unnatural, bodily responses in reaction to each *new* environment in which the body is made to function on its way to perfection. The body does not remain the same in each stage; it changes in each stage. The change in body explains the change in the kind of daemonic warfare. Since the daemons rule the passions, and each environment brings out a different passionate response (i.e. bodily response), the body undergoes social and physical transformation at each stage. The daemons assist the monk to transform that new body in each of its environments. This transformation by daemonic manipulation enables the perfecting of the monk's body.

Each person's body is unique, each daemonic structure is unique, and therefore there can be no universal system for every person to follow in order to become perfect. Every monk must follow the unique way that that particular monk's body requires. The customizing of daemonic attacks discussed above actually signifies the recognition of great diversity among people's constitutions. Since the body is not, as we would perceive it, simply an object with bones, sinews, organs, muscles, tissues, etc., but a creation by angels and daemons who imbue the body with its passions, each passionate and embodied creation is different and different sorts of asceticism are necessary for each one. And if each body is different, each body in each different environment becomes equally diverse and equally in need of particular ascetic activity. Both the material and the social bodies of the monks are subject to ascetical activity.

The daemons enable the monk to construct the monk's new body through the ascetical activity which the presence of the daemons and passions necessitates. The monk, working through the various stages of his bodily transformation, gradually stills the body. The communion of monk with other people, family, other monks, gradually becomes a communion only with the daemons, and finally becomes a communion only with God. The monk's various bodies culminate in the perfect, divinized body. And so the initial distinction between daemon, human, angel, must be adjusted to accommodate one other socialized body, the divinized body of the monk. Because of the daemons' work, the perfected body of the monk hovers above the daemonic and the human, and below the angelic, resting and still and divine.

NOTES

[1] This paper has received the benefit of comments from two different groups: the Ascetic Behavior in Greco-Roman Antiquity research project of the Institute for Antiquity and Christianity (special thanks to Vincent Wimbush, Elizabeth Castelli, Elizabeth Clark, Gail Paterson Corrington, Karen Jo Torjesen, and Kathleen O'Brien Wicker); and a joint symposium on "Daemons in Greek Culture" at the American Philological Association and the Modern Greek Studies Association (special thanks to Charles Stewart, Michael Herzfeld, and Elaine Pagels). Two individuals also read and critiqued the paper: Professor Margaret Miles and Professor Bernadette Brooten, both of Harvard Divinity School. Alas, what remains written here is my own responsibility.

[2] This article intends, as the title indicates, to define monastic daemonology by constructing a separate semantic field for the monastic usage of the word "demon". In order to differentiate this monastic semantic field from others in the "demon" group of fields and in order to avoid the tendency readily to assume that every concept of "demon" is the same, I have retained an older spelling for the word, namely "daemon" (Greek: *daimōn*).

[3] I have chosen three primary monastic texts, representing three different perspectives on the subject: John Climacus, *The Ladder of Divine Ascent* (PG 88: col. 632–1208); the English translation is a revised translation of the earlier translation of Archmandrite Lazarus Moore by the monks of Holy Transfiguration Monastery based upon "the edition of Sophronius Eremites, Constantinope, 1883, and . . . Migne, *Patrologia Graeca*, volume 88. . . . [and] a ninth century manuscript (No. 421) from Mt. Sinai" (p. xviii) (rev. ed.; Boston: Holy Transfiguration Monastery, 1978—the paragraph numbers here refer to Moore's numeration); Pseudo-Athanasius, *The Life and Activity of the Holy and Blessed Teacher Syncletica* (PG 28: cols. 1487–1558); there is an English translation by Elizabeth Castelli in Wimbush:265–311, the translation here, however, is my own adaptation; and Maximus the Confessor, *The Ascetic Discourse* (PG 90: cols 911–958); English translation used throughout this paper is by Polycarp Sherwood (ACW, 21; New York: Newman Press, 1955), see also *Maximus the Confessor: Selected Writings*, trans. George C. Berthold (Classics of Western Spirituality; New York: Paulist Press, 1985). The translation of the *Apocryphon of John* is that of Frederik Wisse in

Robinson:104–123. Climacus' *Ladder* represents a late sixth– or early seventh–century handbook of monastic formation; Syncletica's *Life* is a mid fifth–century instructional biography; and Maximus the Confessor's *Discourse* is a seventh–century exposition of the ascetical life.

[4] It is not, however, a strict demarcation according to ontological status, or a chain of being. In a chain, the body is connected only to the lower realms, while the mind or soul is connected to the higher. Both overlap in the person. But for the monk, the body is perfected, not simply linked to the lower nature or rejected. See argument below.

[5] On the body in gnostic speculation, see the superb article by Michael Williams (1989:141) who writes: "It is striking how frequently Gnostic mythology actually brings in the human anatomy—and especially the sexual anatomy. It is as though many Gnostics saw in the body not only an intimation, a reflection, of a divine Human identity, but a kind of map of reality."

I especially wish to thank Elaine Pagels for her help in clarifying this section of the paper.

[6] It is peculiar that the connection of daemons and the passions, at least in the *Apocryphon of John*, comes about in the creation of the primordial Adam, the higher Adam, not the material Adam created later by the jealous powers. Even if we (or the monks of the monastic tradition) did not identify the monastic "angelic life" with the "primordial Adam" of the gnostic tradition, although the correlation is striking, the passions and the struggle centering on the passions for both the monks and the *Apocryphon of John* signify a higher form of life than the material.

WORKS CONSULTED

Brown, Peter
    1981   *The Cult of the Saints: Its Rise and Function in Latin Christianity.* Chicago: University of Chicago Press.

    1988   *The Body and Society: Men, Women, and Sexual Renunciation in Early Christianity.* New York: Columbia University Press

Burkert, Walter
    1985   *Greek Religion.* Trans. John Raffan. Cambridge: Harvard University Press.

Clark, Elizabeth
    1986a   "Devil's Gateway and Bride of Christ: Women in the Early Christian World." Pp. 23–94 in *Ascetic Piety and Women's Faith: Essays on Late Ancient Christianity.* Lewiston: Edwin Mellen.

    1986b   "John Chrysostom and the Subintroductae." Pp. 265–90 in *Ascetic Piety and Women's Faith: Essays on Late Ancient Christianity.* Lewiston: Edwin Mellen.

    1990   "New Perspectives on the Origenist Controversy: Human Embodiment and Ascetic Strategies." *CH* 59:145–62.

Climacus, John
　1978　*The Ladder of Divine Ascent*. Rev. ed. Boston: Holy Transfiguration Monastery.

Dechow, Jon F.
　1988　*Dogma and Mysticism in Early Christianity: Epiphanius of Cyprus and the Legacy of Origen*. North American Patristic Society Monograph 13. Macon: Mercer University Press.

"Démon"
　1957　Vol. III, col. 141–238. *Dictionaire de Spiritualité*. Paris: Beauchesne.

Dodds, E. R.
　1951　*The Greeks and the Irrational*. Berkeley: University of California Press.
　1965　*Pagan and Christian in an Age of Anxiety*. Cambridge: Cambridge University Press.

Ferguson, Everett
　1987　*Backgrounds of Early Christianity*. Grand Rapids: Eerdmans.

Foerster, Werner
　1964　"*Daimōn*." Trans. G. W. Bromily in *The Theological Dictionary of the New Testament*. II: 1–20. Ed. G. Kittel. Grand Rapids: Eerdmans.

Fowden, Garth
　1982　"The Pagan Holy Man in Late Antique Society." *JHS* 102:33–59.

Geertz, Clifford
　1973　"The Impact of the Concept of Culture on the Concept of Man." Pp. 33–54 in *The Interpretation of Culture: Selected Essays*. New York: Basic Books.

Haraway, Donna
　1989　"The Biopolitics of Postmodern Bodies: Determinations of Self in Immune System Discourse." *Differences: A Journal of Feminist Cultural Studies* 1:3–43.

Harpham, Geoffrey Galt
　1987　*The Ascetic Imperative in Culture and Criticism*. Chicago: University of Chicago Press.

Jones, Alan W.
    1985   *Soul Making: The Desert Way of Spirituality.* San Francisco: Harper and Row.

Jung, Carl Gustav
    1958   "Foreward to Werblowsky's 'Lucifer and Promethius.'" In *Collected Works*, Vol. 11 *Psychology and Religion: West and East.* Bolligen Series XX. Princeton: Princeton University Press.

Kelly, Henry Ansgar
    1974   *The Devil, Demonology and Witchcraft: The Development of Christian Beliefs in Evil Spirits.* Rev. ed. New York: Doubleday.

Kelsey, Morton
    1973   *Healing and Christianity: Healing in Ancient Thought and Modern Times.* New York: Harper and Row.
    1978   *Discernment: A Study in Ecstasy and Evil.* New York: Paulist.

Lakoff, George and Mark Johnson
    1980   *Metaphors We Live By.* Chicago: University of Chicago Press.

Kirschner, Robert
    1984   "The Vocation of Holiness in Late Antiquity." *VC* 38:105–24.

Layton, Bentley
    1987   *The Gnostic Scriptures.* Garden City: Doubleday.

Maximus the Confessor
    1955   *The Ascetic Discours.* Trans. Polycarp Sherwood. ACW. 21. New York: Newman.
    1985   *Maximus the Confessor: Selected Writings.* Trans. George C. Berthold. Classics of Western Spirituality. New York: Paulist.

Michie, Helena
    1987   *The Flesh Made Word: Female Figures and Women's Bodies.* New York: Oxford University Press.

Nouwen, Henri J. M.
    1981   *The Way of the Heart: Desert Spirituality and Contemporary Ministry.* New York: Seabury.

O'Laughlin, Michael
    1987   "Origenism in the Desert: Anthropology and Integration in Evagrius Ponticus." Th. D. Diss. Harvard University

Pagels, Elaine
- 1985 "The Politics of Paradise: Augustine's Exegesis of Genesis 1–3 versus that of John Chrysostom." *HTR* 78:67–99.
- 1986 "Exegesis and Exposition of the Genesis Creation Accounts in Selected Texts from Nag Hammadi." In *Nag Hammadi, Gnosticism, and Early Christianity*. Ed. Charles W. Hedrick and Robert Hodgson. Peabody: Hendrickson.

Robinson, James M., ed.
- 1988 *The Nag Hammadi Library in English*. 3rd ed. San Francisco: Harper and Row

Rouselle, Aline
- 1988 *Porneia: On Desire and the Body in Antiquity*. Ttrans. Felicia Pheasant. Oxford: Blackwell.

Rudolph, Kurt
- 1983 *Gnosis*. Trans. Robert McL. Wilson. New York: Harper and Row.

Russell, Burton
- 1977 *The Devil: Perceptions of Evil from Antiquity to Primitive Christianity*. Ithaca: Cornell University Press.
- 1981 *Satan: The Early Christian Tradition*. Ithaca: Cornell University Press.
- 1984 *Lucifer: The Devil in the Middle Ages*. Ithaca: Cornell University Press.
- 1988 *The Prince of Darkness: Radical Evil and the Power of Good in History*. Ithaca: Cornell University Press.

Theodora, Amma
- 1987 *To Gerontikon ētoi apophthegmata agiōn gerontōn*. Ed. P. B. Paschou. Athens: Astir.

Valantasis, Richard
- 1989 "Adam's Body: Uncovering Esoteric Tradition in the *Apocryphon of John* and Origen's *Diaglogue with Heraclides*." *SecCent* 7:150–62
- 1990 "The Eastern Church's Theme of Deification in Nicholas Cabasilas' *The Life in Christ*." *Studies in Formative Spirituality* 9:89–101.
- 1991 *Spiritual Guides of the Third Century: A Semiotic Study of the Guide-Disciple Relationship in Christianity, Neoplatonism, Her-*

metism, and Gnosticism. Harvard Dissertations in Religions 27. Minneapolis: Fortress.

Wicker, Kathleen O'Brien
"'The Politics of Paradise' Reconsidered: John Chrysostom and Porphyry." [forthcoming]

Williams, Michael
1981 "Stability as a Soteriological Theme in Gnosticism." Vol 2:819–29 in *The Rediscovery of Gnosticism.* Ed. Bentley Layton. Studies in the History of Religion 41. Leiden: Brill.
1985 *The Immoveable Race: A Gnostic Designation and the Theme of Stability in Late Antiquity.* Leiden: Brill.
1989 "Divine Image—Prison of Flesh: Perceptions of the Body in Ancient Gnosticism." Part I. pp. 129–47 in *Fragments for a History of the Human Body.* Ed. Michael Feher. New York: Zone.

Wimbush, Vincent L., ed.
1990 *Ascetic Behavior in Greco-Roman Antiquity: A Sourcebook.* Studies in Antiquity and Christianity. Minneapolis: Fortress.

ASCETIC BEHAVIOR AND COLOR-FUL LANGUAGE: STORIES ABOUT ETHIOPIAN MOSES

Vincent L. Wimbush
Union Theological Seminary
New York City

ABSTRACT

The characterization of the fouth–century Black (Ethiopian) monk named Moses in late ancient Christian hagiographic narratives opens wide a window not only onto particular understandings of, and propaganda about, ascetic piety and religious orientations to the world, but also ancient (non-black) Christian sensitivies to racial/color differences. Four ancient sources—Palladius' *Lausiac History*, Sozomen's *Ecclesiastical History*, the anonymous *Apophthegmata Patrum*, and *Acta Sanctorum*—are analyzed on the basis of a recent translation.

I

Given the nature of their sources, and given the influence and challenges from other fields and disciplines, the fields of ancient studies (including the study of ancient Christianity) are now more than ever forced to question the notion of texts as *simple* sources for historical-reconstructive and historical-interpretive purposes. They are being challenged to engage seriously the problems inherent in relating the study of history and rhetoric, history and textuality, history and the critical study of literature, history and discursive strategies. It seems most useful and appropriate at the outset, rather than attempt to make general comments about how the field of ancient Christianity should draw the lines in such matters, to turn attention to particular motifs and issues in a particular complex of ancient Christian texts that can help focus and problematize the issues so as to provide suggestions for further work.

II

I should like to draw attention to two motifs—racial-color differences and ascetic piety; how the former functions as part of the discursive strategies for the valuation and commendation of the latter in a particular complex of ancient Christian texts; what this function suggests first and foremost about the perspectives and orientations of the writers and collectors of such texts, and what these perspectives and orientations might reveal about the presence and influence of Black African peoples in ancient Christian literature. My discussion is (by design at this point in my own thinking and research) introductory, exploratory and schematic.

In the first paragraph of her essay entitled "Virginity as Metaphor: Women and the Rhetoric of Early Christianity," Averil Cameron makes the following provocative statement about the limited perspectival character of the extant ancient Christian literature and its implications as such for scholarship, including, but not limited to, the study of the presence and influence of women in early Christianity:

> The rhetoric of the early church was a *male* rhetoric, and it is only recently that readings of it have not also been *male* readings. Thus the entire debate about the "position of women in the early church" has taken place, and still must take place, within a framework of *male* textuality (Cameron:184; emphases mine).

In this passage and in subsequent remarks in the same essay Cameron directly addresses the problem of the complex relationship between history and (the rhetoric of the) text by arguing that the most pressing intellectual challenge—even if ultimately the primary concern is for historical-reconstructive work, especially with a view to "setting the record straight" about the role of women in early Christianity—is an examination of the "misogynistic" *rhetoric* of ancient Christian texts.

> "The question of how women really fared in the early Christian world is a second-order question, to be approached only after [examination of] the rhetoric of texts" (185).

Although there are some differences in approaches and nuances, the issue of the Black presence and influence in biblical antiquity, including Near Eastern, Greco-Roman and Christian antiquity, has been raised from a methodological perspective similar to the one regarding the role of women in ancient Christianity. Both issues, for example, obviously arise from those who have been defined as more or less on the margins of established scholarship. There have been numerous critical and not so critical revisionist histories designed to isolate the African influences upon western civilization, including early Christianity (Bernal). Given the history of racism in the West, including western scholarship, and Christianity as part of its ideological arsenal, there should be little wonder that more than the establishment of the "facts" is and has been at stake in debate about the African presence and influences in biblical traditions. Nevertheless, most critical scholars—African, African American and others—will acknowledge the complexity and problematic nature of the issue, especially the extent to which we are dependent upon *literary* sources.

Since Christianity has almost from the beginning been a literary phenomenon, we are quite dependent upon literary sources for answers to most of our basic questions about it. This includes the question about the Black African presence and influence in ancient Christianity, as well as fundamental questions about Christian self-definitions and orientations. For such questions examination of different rhetorical strategies may provide a helpful heuristic key and a most useful beginning.

This essay cannot possibly explore all of the rhetorical strategies that may be discernible in early Christian literature; it is designed only to be a springboard for further research and discussion by focusing upon one example of a discursive strategy that involves the interfacing of the *rhetoric* of racial-color differences and the *rhetoric* of ascetic piety. Such a strategy as part of an effort to commend ascetic piety is likely not only to contribute to a better understanding of the phenomenon of asceticism in Christian antiquity, it might also provide a clearer understanding of the methodological challenges involved in an effort to understand among other topics the Black presence and influence in early Christianity. This is, at any rate, the aim of the present essay. Since ascetic behavior can with justification be viewed as reflective of specific types of orientations to and understandings of the world and of the self in the world, literary strategies that attempt to persuade readers of the value of ascetic behaviors very much need to be understood. Such a strategy that is found to make use of the rhetoric of, and draw upon reactions to, racial-color differences represents a fascinating find, begging serious consideration.

III

The are very few actual references to Black peoples in ancient Christian texts. Where there are such references they are often pregnant with symbolism, often to emphasize, at the expense of credulity, the universality of Christian salvation (cf. e.g. Acts 8:26–40; Snowden; Courtes). Such few references "work" the symbolism far too much to be accepted as unproblematized recording of social (viz. interracial) dynamic and history.

References in Greek and Roman literature to the color "black" without direct connection to Black people are much more numerous. These references also are used symbolically. Such symbolism is in fact so pervasive that it makes much more complex the matter of the Black presence and influence in antiquity, including Christian antiquity. The situation certainly warrants the serious study of the *language* of color differences, no matter whether the goal be to clarify the "historical record" regarding racial diversity, or to understand more about aspects of ancient sensibilities and mentalities.

Augustine's statements about color differences serve as an example of the popular ancient Christian symbolization and spiritualization of color:

> Ask yourself what sort of servant you really value. You may have a servant who is handsome, tall, and finely built, but a thief, a rogue and a swindler; and you may have another who is dwarfish, ill-featured, and foul-skinned [*colore tetro*], but trustworthy, thrifty, and steady. Now which of these two, I ask you, do you really value? If you judge by the eyes in your head, the one who is handsome but dishonest wins: if by the eyes of your heart, the one who is ugly but reliable (Augustine, Second Discourse on Psalm 33:15, *Ennarrationes in Psalmos*; cited by Frost:2)

And in an obvious reflection upon the provocative pre-Pauline primitive Christian theme struck by the apostle Paul in Galatians 3:28 (Meeks: 88, 155), to the effect that old human types and divisions—"Jew and Gentile," "Greek and barbarian," "slave and free," "male and female"—are "put off" in the ritual of baptism:

> ... whoever is born anywhere as a human being, that is, as a rational mortal creature, however strange he may appear to our senses in bodily form or color or motion or utterance, in any faculty, part or quality of his nature whatsoever, let no true believer have any doubt that such an individual is descended from the one who was first created (*de civitate Dei* 16.8; cited by Frost:2)

Such sentiments were part of and need to be understood in light of the ancient aristocratic Greek and Greco-Roman and Christian ethos that tended toward the relativizing, even rejection, of (accidental) worldly goods, attributes, situations and circumstances, in light of increased emphasis on the cultivation of the self, the mind (*nous*) and the spiritual (*pneumatika*). With beginnings among aristocratic intellectuals in the Greek classical period, such an ethos emphasized the absolute superiority of the intellectual and spiritual over all other pursuits and interests, all worldly situations and circumstances. The (socio-economic-political) consequences of such intellectualizing and spiritualizing sentiments and interpretations for many in ancient societies was often the maintenance of the status quo—to the clear advantage of aristocrats, the disadvantage of all others prone to receive the pronouncements of elites as truth.

The example of slavery is the clearest and most dramatic example from history of the effects of the aristocratic spiritualizing and intellectualizing ethos and its rhetoric. Although the topos did not begin with him, Aristotle is probably the most influential figure from the Greek classical period in the debate about "natural slavery," whether some human beings—notably non-Greeks, *barbaroi*—are slaves by nature (de Ste.

Croix:417 n. 17). I agree with de Ste. Croix (417) that statements made by Aristotle establish in a powerful way the intellectualist, spiritualizing ethos that led to the socio-economic-political "non-reality" of slavery. It is a fateful argument that, along with others, provides ideological basis for the relativizing of the world in the Hellenistic and late antique periods, and helps account for the ancient Christian adoption of such an ethos (409–52).

> ... [H]e is by nature a slave who is capable of belonging to another (and that is why he does so belong), and who participates in reason [*logou*] so far as to apprehend it but not to possess it.... [T]here exist certain persons who are essentially slaves everywhere and certain others who are so nowhere. And the same applies also about nobility: our nobles consider themselves noble not only in their own country but everywhere, but they think that barbarian noblemen are only noble in their own country—which implies that there are two kinds of nobility and of freedom, one absolute and the other relative ... in so speaking they make nothing but virtue and vice the distinction between slave and free, the noble and the base-born.... [I]n some instances it is not the case that one set are slaves and the other freemen by nature; and also that in some instances such a distinction does exist, when slavery for the one and mastership for the other are advantageous, and it is just and proper for the one party to be governed and for the other to govern by the form of government for which they are by nature fitted ... (*Pol.* I.2.13, 18–19).

The ancient Christian sources that draw directly upon the intellectualist and spiritualizing ethos and in which the more heuristically fruitful references to color differences are found—for the sake of addressing both historical and literary questions—are among different types of narrative materials. Narrative, part of the "literature of edification" of ancient Christianity, has been argued to be a most appropriate and powerful propaganda tool for ascetic piety (Harpham: 67f.). It is among a certain cluster of narrative forms—historical, hortatory, panegyric writings—where we find an interesting combination of intellectualist color symbolism, through the eulogistic characterization of a Black person, and the commendation of a type of ascetic piety. This total combination is so rare for the literature of antiquity in general that it begs attention. Moreover, because my interest has for some time encompassed both ascetic piety of the type in evidence here and the Black presence and influence in early Christianity as separate issues, the literature that allows both to be taken up cannot possibly be ignored.

IV

Ethiopian Moses, or Moses the Black, is characterized as an ideal monk in four ancient sources—Palladius' *Lausiac History* (c. 420); Sozomen's *Ecclesiastical History* (c. 443–448); the anonymous *Apophthegmata*

Patrum (late 6th century); and *Acta Sanctorum* (10th century).[1] In many ways these represent typical hagiographic texts from ancient Christianity. Kathleen Wicker's examination of the sources has recently led her to conclude that the Moses characterization functioned variously to commend the ascetic lifestyle as the superior lifestyle (Palladius, Sozomen), to instruct and edify those who have accepted the monastic life (*Apoph. Patr.*), and to provide a model of monastic perfection (*Acta Sanc.*) (Wicker:333).

Wicker also argues that these sources "reflect" perceptions of racial-color differences in antiquity. In their "histories" addressed to literate audiences far away from Africa, Palladius and Sozomen, Wicker suggests, seemed unconcerned about the issue of Moses' color. Moses is simply noted as an "Ethiopian," a Black African. The *Apoph. Patr.* and *Act. Sanct.*, because they contain explicit valuations based on Moses' color, are said to reflect contemporary attitudes about racial-color differences in Egypt and throughout the Greco-Roman world (334).

Although I would make the same basic divisions among the four text-sources, I would nuance the arguments so as to make it clear that all of the texts more or less reflect the same (white or non-black) perspective regarding racial-color differences (especially, the color, black). The difference between the first category of (seemingly benign) texts and the second category of (more explicitly prejudiced) texts lies only in *literary* strategy. All of the texts reflect a view of Moses *on account of his color* as "other," as alien, as polar opposite. This perspective is consistent with classical and post-classical references to Black Africans (Cortes). *Apart from his color there is no reason for the stories, first oral, then written, about Moses.* His heroic ascetic piety was not singular. His ascetic piety provided such a perfect counterpoint (He's too good to be true!) to (the white, non-black view of) his color that it would normally—given the usual logic and scepticism of historical and literary criticism—cast great doubt about the historicity of Moses. The point should be, however, that differences between the text-sources about him should be seen as differences in the sophistication of literary strategy, not in real attitudes about color differences. The Moses story itself, in whatever version, was not about a pious man who happened to be Black; it was about a *Black* man whose blackness alone was important. The latter served as a symbol of all forms of lower, imperfect existence that were other than, and in *polar opposition* to, the the ideal religious life, *viz.* the ascetic life.

Palladius's initial identification of Moses as "Ethiopian by birth," and "black," functioned to explain, and provide dramatic narrative effect for, further characterization of him as recalcitrant slave, robber and murderer. The apologetic nature of the "history" is clearly set forth: "I am obliged," says Palladius, "to tell about his wicked behavior in order to demonstrate the excellence of his conversion." Moses' "wicked behavior" is all the more onerous and dramatic because he is black, the "other," the assumed polar opposite of the visualized good. The conversion of such a man was thought to be good drama, enough to sell the reader on the ascetic life.

According to Sozomen's account, which was clearly dependent upon Palladius's account, "Moses the Ethiopian" was before conversion a man of ill repute. So disreputable was he considered that it was said that "no one else ever made such a change from evil to excellence," that is, to "the height of monastic philosophy." That the pre-conversion Moses could be considered to have been so radically and uniquely notorious can be understood not only as propaganda for the ascetic lifestyle, but also a sharing of strong assumptions and prejudices regarding Ethiopians between writer and intended audience. Direct prejudicial statements were not, therefore, required for the story; only the mention of Moses as Ethiopian, with the underlying assumption that something (viz., being black) about being Ethiopian made one different was required.

The very late (tenth century) and anonymous writing entitled "The Life of Moses The Ethiopian" obviously drew from earlier sources, and reflected the ascetic (viz. monastic) traditions and values of the time. (330 n 9). Its importance for us lies in its rather clear reflection of the ancient well-springs and western historical trajectory of the assumption that being Ethiopian and Black represented otherness, foreignness, from the perspective of non-blacks.

The efforts to include Ethiopian Moses in the economy of salvation are much too nuanced and clever for comfort (*pace* Snowden:169–95; cf. Wicker:334 n. 37). Moses as an Ethiopian is seen as representative of a far distant and strange people, in the same way that Scythians are seen as a far distant people in the opposite direction.

> "The kingdom of God has not been closed to slaves or evildoers, but they are within it who, as is fitting, have made use of repentance and prefer to live righteously and according to God. And it has by no means been closed to Scythians or Ethiopians." (*Acta Sanct.* 1; Wicker:344)

The contrasting of Moses' skin color and slave status with his ascetic piety is consistent and striking: "He ... who had a black-skinned body, acquired a soul more brilliant than the rays of the sun." He was said to be "vulgar and worthless," "wayward and ignorant" (*Act. Sanct.* 2; Wicker: 344). But after having been touched by "divine grace," and having joined the ascetic life, he became "pitiful in appearance, abject in manner, contrite in spirit, totally restrained ..." (*Act. Sanct.* 4; Wicker: 345). At first sight of him the other monks, all of whom we must assume to be non-black, were afraid. But the fervency of his contrition and piety matched or countered the "blackness" of his sins, symbolized by his skin color. This as the moral of the story is made unmistakably clear:

> As infamous as he was for evil, so greatly did he shine as an expert in perfection.... Moses was indeed a great monk, and was talked about by everyone. The desert, the mountains, the city, and all the surrounding areas resounded with Moses, Moses, Moses. And here it seems to me that Moses alone has changed his appearance, even though an Ethiopian is never completely washed clean. For indeed, he cleansed his soul, if not his body, with the hyssop of repentance, and he made it more brilliant than the sparkling suns... (*Act. Sanct.* 6; Wicker: 346).

The anonymous sixth-century alphabetical collection of the *Apoph. Patr.* is in many ways the most important of the sources about Moses. Intended for the edification of monks, it includes the most powerful connection between color symbolism and ascetic piety. The popular prejudice against Ethiopians is made clear in the contemptuous question "Why has this Ethiopian come into our midst?" Such a question is used by the editor to point to and counterpose the rigor and constancy of the ascetic piety of the Black man called Moses. The more he is hassled by the other (white) monks, the more exemplary he becomes as an ascetic: "I was troubled but I did not say anything" (*Apoph. Patr.* 3; Wicker: 339).

Indication of the view of blackness and of Moses as Black man who is also convert and fellow monk and cleric can be found in the statement the archbishop is made to speak upon laying the tunic upon Moses: "Behold, you have become completely white, Father Moses." In the response Moses is made to give,—"Indeed, the outside, O Lord Father; would that the inside were also white,"—the point that the ascetic life signifies radical transformation or change of identity is made most dramatically through the employment of color symbolism and color contrast.

More officially sanctioned hassling of Moses on account of his racial and color difference ensues and Moses again accepts such treatment with humility characteristic of the ascetic: "Rightly have they treated you, ash skin, black one. As you are not a man, why should you come among men?" (*Apoph. Patr.* 45; Wicker: 340). Because Moses was a Black man— from the perspective of the editor and audience assumed to be odd, even to be held in contempt—the point of the story is to emphasize how very pious he was as an ascetic. As pious an ascetic as he was considered foreign and different. And his foreignness was on account of his skin color.

V.
Summary Conclusions

The color symbolism in the stories told, transmitted and written about Moses point to provocative questions and suggestions to be pursued regarding at least two important issues—(1) the presence and views of Blacks in Christian antiquity from the perspective of non-Blacks; and (2) the motives and self-understandings reflected in certain forms of ascetic behavior among non-Blacks.

The texts about Moses suggest that the ancient Christians followed a widespread trend among Greeks and Romans with respect to color symbolism (Courtes; Snowden; Steidle). The texts at first glance suggest that Black peoples in particular were included within the circle of the elect without problem. On more careful reading, however, it appears that Moses *as a Black man* was much too important a symbol of the superiority of ascetic piety to be beyond doubt as to whether he was an historical figure, or as to whether his characterization in the stories reflects ancient Christian racial inclusiveness (*contra* Snowden). In other words, the stories are worked too hard by different communities and traditions to reflect *both* the attractiveness and superiority of the ascetic life *and* the simple openness and inclusiveness on the part of Christian—especially monastic—communities. The problem lies in the fact that not only is the symbolism rather heavy and thick—almost too nuanced (again, Moses being *too* good to be true; the opposites *too* radical)—not only is Black Moses *rare* among early Christian spiritual athletes and heroes as preserved in the oral and written legacies of ancient Christianity, but the advancement of the attractiveness and superiority of the ascetic life is done at the expense of Moses, not just as individual, but as representative of Black peoples.

The texts and their use of Moses and color symbolism would seem at first to suggest a reading of monastic ascetic piety as radical, as defined by totalities and absolutes, radical opposites—the world (and for some, including even other tamer Christian [=ascetic] lifestyles) against those who have adopted the monastic-ascetic lifestyle. The radical opposition of the color "black" against the color "white" in general, and Moses as living example of black peoples and their assumed sinful state and "other-ness," served well the advancement of a certain type of ascetic propaganda. The ascetic lifestyle seems to be associated with the adoption of radical commitment, the living of life in radical discipleship, an orientation to the world that spelled distance, critique, resistance. This ascetic orientation to the world was understood to parallel the foreignness that dark-skinned peoples were considered to represent by those transmitting the tradition to experience.

Yet it is important not to fall uncritically under the aesthetic discursive strategy that is in the working of the symbolism in these texts to the point that *historical* dynamic, and realities are forgotten (Palmer). To be sure, asceticism as valorized in the literary characterization of Moses was supposed to be histrionic, stark and radical. But in the employment of such symbolism in literary form the ascetic communities and traditions behind the texts reflect aspects of certain types of historical-political realities, prejudices and sensibilities. They betray the extent to which certain ascetic communities were not, actually could not have been, otherworldly (and apolitical!), according to popular notions and much scholarly argumentation regarding the "religious" life. Such communities accepted widespread cultural concepts, assumptions and prejudices, and even attempted to advance their cause by playing upon (actually texturing) such.

The lesson here is not that religious people were or could be found to be hypocritical or less than perfect—or something of the kind. The important lesson is that the literary games played with asceticism and loss of world, with their use of color symbolism, can tell us something about *history* and *discursive strategies*, about mentalities, or visions of the world in history and how they come to expression.

Through the color-coded discourses about asceticism we can learn much about the character of the *worldliness* of a particular *loss-of-world* ethos and its corresponding required behavior. From a reading of the texts about Moses, asceticism cannot be considered world-rejection in any absolute apolitical sense. It must be understood as a type of world-orientation involving selected renunciation, or reprioritization of the world, complete with selected cultural (even minority culturalist) and political assumptions and prejudices. This insight of course squares with the notion that ascetic behavior is not simply rejection of the world, but involves the embracing of an ideal (Fraade). The color symbolism in the Moses texts points the reader to the importance of seeking to discover and account for the *worldly* choices of renunciation.

NOTES

[1] I owe gratitude to my friend and Claremont colleague Kathleen O. Wicker not only for her collection and translation of the relevant sources, but also for her encouragement of my interpretive efforts.

WORKS CONSULTED

Aristotle
　1927　　*Politics*. Trans., with an introduction and notes by H. Rackham. Cambridge: Harvard University.

Bernal, Martin
　1987　　*Black Athena: The Afroasiatic Roots of Classical Civilization*. vol. 1. London: Free Association Books.

Cameron, Averil
　1990　　"Virginity as Metaphor: Women and the Rhetoric of Early Christianity." In *History as Text*. Ed. A. Cameron. Chapel Hill: University of North Carolina Press.

Courtes, Jean Marie
　1979　　"The Theme of 'Ethiopians' in Patristic Literature." In *The Image of the Black in Western Art*. Vol. II.1. By Jean Devisse. Gen. Ed. L. Bugner. Tr. William Granger Ryan. New York: William Morrow and Company.

De Ste. Croix, G. E. M.
　1981　　*The Class Struggle in the Ancient Greek World: From the Archaic Age to the Arab Conquests*. Ithaca: Cornell University Press.

Felder, Cain, ed.
　1991　　*Stony the Road We Trod: African American Interpretation*. Minneapolis: Fortress.

Fraade, Steven D.
　1986　　"Ascetical Aspects of Ancient Judaism." In *Jewish Spirituality: From the Bible Through the Middle Ages*. Vol. 13 of *World Spirituality: An Encyclopedic History of the Religious Quest*. New York: Crossroad.

Frost, Peter
　1991　　"Attitudes Toward Blacks in the Early Christian Era." *Second Century* 8.1:1–11.

Meeks, Wayne A.
　1983　　*The First Urban Christians: The Social World of the Apostle Paul*. New Haven: Yale University.

Palmer, Bryan D.
1990 *Descent into Discourse: The Reification of Language and the Writing of Social History*. Philadelphia: Temple University Press.

Snowden, Frank M., Jr.
1970 *Blacks in Antiquity: Ethiopians in the Greco-Roman Experience*. Cambridge: Harvard University Press.

Steidle, P. Basilius
1958 "Der 'schwarze kleine Knabe' in der alten Mönchserzählung." In *Benedictinische Monatschrift* 34: 339–350.

Wicker, Kathleen O.
1990 "Ethiopian Moses (Collected Sources)." Pp. 329–48 in *Ascetic Behavior in Greco-Roman Antiquity: A Source Book*. Ed. Vincent L. Wimbush. Minneapolis: Fortress.

IV

ASCESIS, AUTHORITY, AND TEXT:
THE ACTS OF THE COUNCIL OF SARAGOSSA

Virginia Burrus
Drew University
The Theological School

ABSTRACT

It is frequently claimed that the *Acts of the Council of Saragossa* reflect the viewpoints of an anti-ascetic episcopacy confronted with the influence of Priscillian and other ascetics in late fourth-century Spain. This study, in contrast, attempts to highlight the ascetic aspects of the understanding of Christian lifestyle and authority articulated by the Saragossan council. I propose that the conflict underlying the *Acts* can profitably be viewed as a conflict not between asceticism and its opponents, but rather between divergent understandings of asceticism which in turn undergird divergent understandings of authority. By broadening our use of the category of asceticism and the subcategories of cenobitism and eremitism, we enhance our understanding of the process by which ascetic and episcopal authority were joined in the late antique Christian West. We also observe the significant role played by the genre of conciliar *acta* in that process, alongside the more commonly acknowledged role of the *vitae* of ascetic bishops.

Introduction

Disturbing new practices were threatening the unity and stability of the Spanish churches—at least so it seemed to the twelve bishops who met in Saragossa in the year 380. The *Acts of the Council of Saragossa* present the practices of Christian ascetics through the eyes of their opponents in the moment of first encounter. Lacking any technical terminology of asceticism, the council struggles to classify the troubling phenomena, ultimately locating the source of its outrage in a perceived disregard for the ecclesiastical hierarchy. The council's eight official rulings—presented in the form of a dramatic enactment of episcopal authority—conjure the image of a deviant and insubordinate lifestyle which necessitates the stern judgments of the bishops. The text's historical *reliability* is questionable on a number of points: the implicit characterization of the Spanish Christians who observe the offensive practices, the claimed unanimity of the gathered bishops, and the implied effectiveness of the episcopal sanctions. But the text's historical *function* in asserting and thereby strengthening the authority of the episcopacy is clear. This act of assertion represents more than a defense of the *status quo*: in formulating its opposition to the Spanish ascetics, the council simultaneously engages in a subtle redefinition of episcopal authority.

The conflicting understandings of authority which underlie the literary strategies of the *Acts of the Council of Saragossa* are embedded in different emerging ascetic orientations. The bishops at Saragossa oppose one set of ascetic practices. In its place, they advocate an alternative lifestyle of discipline and order focused on obedience to episcopal authority and the renunciation of personal desires and private pursuits. They present their opponents as having succumbed to the temptations of self-glorification. While we more easily identify the individualistically oriented practices of those opponents as "ascetic," the bishops too attempt to define a life of Christian discipline. The *Acts of the Council of Saraogossa* is not, therefore, a fundamentally anti-ascetic text—as has often been claimed (e.g. Vollman: 498)—but rather a text which engages the question of the true nature of Christian discipline and authority.

This repositioning of the *Acts* in relation to the phenomenon we describe as "asceticism" may seem to involve an irrelevant quibble over terminology—or worse yet, a disturbingly broad redefinition of a formerly precise and useful term. I hope to show, however, that a fresh look at the category of asceticism may prove beneficial not only for our understanding of the phenomenon of asceticism in general, but also for our understanding of the historical development of late antique Christianity and of the role which certain kinds of texts played in that development. By acknowledging the ascetic aspect of the episcopally centered ecclesiology and the cathedral liturgy which emerge in this period, we avoid an overly simplistic opposition between "asceticism" and the "ecclesiastical hierarchy," and we are thereby in a better position to understand not only the development of a celibate clergy but also the ultimate compatibility of the episcopacy and monastic asceticism in the Christian West. In addition, by identifying the genre of conciliar *acta* not only as a vehicle for the assertion of episcopal authority but also as a form of ascetic discourse, we are able to appreciate the role of such *acta* in the articulation of an ascetic authority of the bishop.

Discussion of the Text

The "transcript of the decisions of the bishops of the Saragossan council of October 4, 380," as the document is entitled, opens with a prefatory clause which sets the scene of the council, identifying the place of meeting and the episcopal participants. As in most documents of the genre, the recorded opinions of the council which follow reflect the language and procedures of senatorial decision-making, above all in the statement of acclamation which seals the final opinion of the council on a given issue: "*Placet*.... It is agreed...." (Hess: 29–32). There are, however, two somewhat unusual formal aspects of the document. First, the *Acts* are published in the form of procedural minutes, not having been transposed from direct discourse into the indirect and more formulaic language commonly used for the pronouncement of a council's judgments (Hess: 25–26, 35–38). The document thus retains a kind of dramatic intensity and immediacy. At the same time, the *Acts* are presented as a transcript not of the proceedings of the entire council but only of the final reading and approval of the council's recorded decisions. They thus depict the council at its most decisive and unanimous moment and avoid identifying the individual bishops who proposed each problem and solution. In place of the individual speakers we hear only the impersonal voice of the secretary Bishop Lucius, who reads the previously recorded opinions aloud, and the anonymous unanimity of "all the bishops," who respond in agreement. This paradoxical combination of dramatic immediacy and anonymous unanimity maximizes the voice of senatorial authority to which all ancient conciliar acts lay claim.

The first of the bishops' eight recorded decisions is targeted at women:

> All women who are of the Catholic church and faithful are to be separated from the reading and meetings of strange men...
>
> *Ut mulieres omnes ecclesiae catholicae et fideles a virorum alienorum lectione et coetibus separentur*...

With the intensifying qualifiers which are piled onto the named target of "women," the bishops move immediately to delineate the boundary between insiders and outsiders and to communicate an implicit threat: if you are a faithful woman, a catholic woman, you will observe this ruling; otherwise, you stand beyond the pale of the catholic faith. Further emotional content is carried by the adjective "strange," which raises the specter of women meeting with non-familial men and thereby invokes the authority of deeply embedded conceptions of female virtue and honor in order to excite moral outrage at the implied violation of women's essential privacy.

The bishops' ruling does not end with this initial command but continues as follows:

> ... but other [women] are to meet with those [women] who read, in pursuit of either teaching or learning, because the Apostle commands this.
>
> ... *vel ad ipsas legentes aliae studio vel docendi vel discendi conveniant, quoniam hoc Apostolus iubet.*

Here women are urged to study in the company of literate women rather than to attend study groups with male readers, where they might presume not only to learn but also to teach. Having evoked the image of insubordinate heretical women mingling scandalously with unrelated men, the council seeks not to prohibit but to redirect the ascetic zeal for study. Study of the scriptures is encouraged, as long as the separation and subordination of the genders is observed in the Christian community. The probable scriptural reference to to 1 Cor 14.34 or 1 Tim 2.12 supports the episcopally sanctioned social order. The bishops close this first ruling by threatening potential transgressors with the vague but severe punishment of anathematization.

The second decision, like the first, is structured in two parts:

> One is not to fast on Sunday, for the sake of the day or belief or superstition; or, rather, those who persist in these opinions are not to be absent from the churches during Lent, nor to lurk in the hiding places of cells and mountains, but they are to keep the example and precept of the bishops, and they are not to meet on strange estates in order to hold meetings.

> *Ne quis ieiunet die Dominica causa temporis aut persuasionis aut suppersitionis; aut de quadragesimarum die ab ecclesiis non desint nec habitent latibula cubiculorum ac montium qui in his suspicionibus perseverant, sed exemplum et praeceptum custodiant sacerdotum, et ad alienas villas agendorum conventuum causa conveniant.*

There are a number of difficulties in interpreting this passage, but I take the phrase "those who persist in these opinions" to refer back to those who fast on Sunday, and I therefore understand the second series of clauses as an emendation of the initial prohibition. That is to say, the council first attempts to dissuade Christians from fasting on Sunday by prohibiting the practice and casting vague aspersions on its motivations. The bishops then back off somewhat from their initial stark prohibition. Their main concern is that the targeted Christians, whether or not they continue to fast on Sunday (during Lent only?), should *not* withdraw from the episcopal congregation during Lent. Rather, the council urges, Christians are to follow the Lenten observances exemplified and commanded by the bishop. Again, the purpose is not to prohibit but to redirect ascetic discipline. Those who withdraw from the congregation are described in terms which invoke the image of the seditious gatherings of Manichees or other political or religious sectarians: *superstitio, latibula, conventus*. Like the women who mix with "strange" men, these Christians gather on "strange" estates, holding secret meetings in places they have no business frequenting. As in the first ruling, potential transgressors are threatened with anathematization.

The third decision is briefer and simpler in structure than either of the first two:

> If someone is proved not to have consumed the grace of the eucharist received in church, let that one be anathema in perpetuity.
>
> *Eucharistiae gratiam si quis probatur acceptam in ecclesia non sumpsisse, anathema sit in perpetuum.*

The problem here lies with those Christians who attend the eucharistic assembly but do not partake of the elements with the rest of the congregation. In opposing this practice, the council seeks to distinguish sharply between insiders and outsiders and, as in the second decision, to restrict those who would create an elite subgroup within the episcopally led community. The severity of the threatened punishment—perpetual anathema—is striking and points to the central importance placed on the eucharist in defining the episcopally focused community of Christians.

The fourth decision is closely parallel to the second in structure, wording, and content:

> On the twenty-one days from December seventeenth to Epiphany, which is the sixth of January—on these continuous days, let no one be allowed to be absent from the church: they are not to be concealed in houses, nor to stay on estates, nor to head for the mountains, nor to walk with bare feet, but to flock to the church.
>
> *Viginti et uno die quo a sextodecimo Kalendas Januarias usque in diem epiphaniae, qui est octavo Idus Januarias, continuis diebus nulli liceat de ecclesia absentare nec latere in domibus nec sedere ad villas nec montes petere nec nudis pedibus incedere, sed concurrere ad ecclesiam.*

Evidently some Christians were observing practices of withdrawal during the pre-Epiphany season similar to the Lenten practices opposed in the council's second decision. The council in turn advocates attendance at daily services during the three weeks before Epiphany: on these continuous days, they declare, Christians are to come together in church. The careful identification of the pre-Epiphany season implies, as the paucity of external evidence seems to confirm, that many were unfamiliar with the custom of observing this Advent period of penitence. It is possible that the council initiates such observances partially in competition with the ascetic practices condemned in the ruling. As in the third ruling, the bishops here threaten perpetual anathematization to transgressors. The discrepancy between this and the lighter punishment meted out in the second ruling probably derives more from the emotional flow of the meeting than from any perceived difference in the severity of the transgressions.

The fifth decision addresses the issue of episcopal solidarity—or the lack thereof:

> Those who through the instruction or decision of a bishop have been separated from the church are not to be received by other bishops. If bishops do this knowingly, let them not have communion.
>
> *Ut ii qui per disciplinam aut sententiam episcopi ab ecclesia fuerint separati, ab aliis episcopis non sint recipiendi. Quod si scientes episcopi fecerint, non habeant communionem.*

The strident cry of "anathema!" is here replaced with the more neutral reference to communion withheld, and there is no explicit mention of deposition. Nevertheless, the decision represents an aggressive move to enforce episcopal compliance with the council's rulings. While the problems created by episcopal disunity were by no means new, no previous council had dared threaten excommunication to bishops who failed to enforce the rulings of their colleagues (cf. Elvira [309] can. 53; Arles [314] can. 17; Nicea [325] can. 5; Antioch [341] can. 6; Sardica [343] can. 13). The intensity of the Saragossan bishops' concern with this issue belies the unanimity implied in the repeated affirmation of "all the bishops" to each of the council's decisions.

The sixth decision is likewise targeted at members of the clergy:

> If one of the clerics leaves his office of his own will on account of presumed luxury and vanity and wants to seem to be some sort of observer of the law in a monastic lifestyle, rather than a cleric, he must thus be driven away from the church; unless he makes amends by beseeching and begging many times, he is not to be received.
>
> *Si quis de clericis propter luxum vanitatemque praesumptam de officio suo sponte discesserit ac se velut observatorem legis in monacho videri voluerit esse quam clericum, ita de ecclesia repellendum ut, nisi rogando atque obsecrando plurimis temporibus satisfecerit, non recipiatur.*

It is not clear whether the targeted offenders are actually abandoning their clerical office or are merely redefining their understandings of the lifestyle and duties appropriate to that office. Regardless of the actual position of the monastic clergy, the Saragossan bishops clearly wish to set up a strong opposition between the rightful clergy and those living "in a monastic lifestyle." The monks follow "their own will" and abandon their duty to their congregations; they pronounce judgment against the established church for its vanity of luxurious living; and they want to to appear superior to the other clergy in their observance of the law. The bishops are outraged by the monks' arrogance, their audacious choice to cultivate their personal virtue rather than to serve the bishop and his community dutifully. Such a "presumption" is itself "vanity." The punishment threatened evokes powerful visual imagery: the monks are not to be "anathematized" or "excommunicated" but rather "driven out of the church"; they are only to be received back by the bishop if they have "beseeched and begged" him repeatedly, concretely symbolizing their acceptance of their subordination to the bishop and the needs of the congregation.

The seventh and eighth decisions continue to address situations of tension arising from competition between various forms of leadership recognized in the Spanish churches. The seventh sets out to restrict the authority of independent "teachers."

> One is not to take for oneself the name of teacher, except those persons to whom it has been granted, according to what has been written.
>
> *Ne quis doctoris sibi nomen imponat praeter has personas quibus concessum est, secundum quod scriptum est.*

Here too the bishops hint at an inappropriate presumption or assertion of self which constitutes a form of disobedience. The vagueness of the language and the unwillingness of the bishops to threaten any punishment to potential offenders indicates that the Saragossan council is treading on thin ice in opposing the authority of independent teachers. Who might legitimately grant the authority implied in the title of "teacher"? The implication is that it is the bishop's right, but this is not explicitly claimed. The invocation of scripture is likewise vague and unpersuasive; if the reference is to Matt 23.8, which restricts the title of "teacher" to Jesus, it seems to contradict the council's assertion that some Christians have been legitimately granted the title. The bishops know that the authority to teach is popularly granted to certain men and women possessing particular education or insight or eloquence. They do not attempt to oppose this authority altogether but rather to subordinate it more firmly to the bishop and the episcopally led congregation.

The council's note of tentativeness persists in its final decision:

> Virgins who have dedicated themselves to God should not be veiled unless of proven age of forty years, which the priest shall confirm.
>
> *Non velandas esse virgines quae se Deo voverint, nisi XL annorum probata aetate quam sacerdos comprobaverit.*

This ruling seeks to establish a distinction—probably a novel distinction—between two categories of Christian virgins: the veiled and the unveiled. It restricts the category of the veiled to those who are at least forty years old and further specifies that the age limit is to be enforced by the bishop. The council's intention seems to be to limit severely the number of publicly honored ascetic women and to exert some degree of episcopal control over those women. Again, no punishment is specified, and the assertion of episcopal control only in the area of confirmation of the age requirement appears remarkably restrained. It is likely that here again the bishops cannot realistically expect—and perhaps do not want—anything more than a formal acknowledgement of their right to exercise authority over the virgins.

The Two Asceticisms

The text presents certain ascetic practices as the source of an informal authority which threatens the ecclesiastical hierarchy. It thus presents the practitioners themselves as arrogant and insubordinate rebels: they gather in secret conventicles and hold themselves aloof from the rest of the congregation; the women among them mingle promiscuously with strange men and usurp authority appropriate to men; some desert their clerical duties, following their own wills and presuming themselves superior to others; others grasp at the title and authority of teacher even without official sanction; and still others claim the public honor of the virgin's veil regardless of their age and without the consent of their bishop. The council calls these rebels to obedience. The assembled bishops threaten to withhold communion from any of their colleagues who condone the subversive practices. They assert the exclusive legitimacy of their own discipline and authority.

Behind the polemical distortions, the *Acts* allow glimpses of the actual lifestyle of the Christians whom the Saragossan bishops opposed. These Christians remained part of their urban congregations, some of them even numbering among the clergy of those congregations. Within their congregations, they strove for a perfect discipline of life which was not common to all. They met in small study groups to read scripture. They fasted on days when some other Christians feasted. They may have preferred not to share the eucharistic elements with their less disciplined brothers and sisters. They withdrew periodically from the life of the city and the urban congregation, especially during seasons of penitence and preparation before Epiphany and Easter: some of them simply practiced solitude in their own homes or estates, others sought out the wilderness, and still others gathered on the estate of some rural patron. Some presumed to criticize the more worldly members of their church and its leadership—whether explicitly or only implicitly by the life they led. Their lifestyle was not uniform or formally organized yet they shared some common practices and goals and beliefs and probably some sense of community. Within this context, it was natural for the ascetics to acknowledge the authority not only of bishops and other official leaders of the church but also of other men and women who distinguished themselves by their disciplined lives or knowledge of scripture or eloquence in expounding the scripture; in fact, it was in the latter group that they tended to identify their true leaders.

Those who gathered at Saragossa agreed that the Christian life was essentially a life of discipline, constant striving against temptation, and continual self-denial. However, they perceived in the practices of their opponents not a praiseworthy ascesis but an acquiescence to the temptations of self-aggrandizement and the dangers of an arrogant individualism. Opposing the call to the perfection and exaltation of an individual life, those who gathered at Saragossa urged Christians to seek, rather, to identify with the community and conform to its ordered pattern of human relations. They were not to withdraw into the dangerous realm of solitude but to "flock to the church," to become one with their community in the sharing of the body and blood of Christ, in the common adherence to "the example and precept of the bishop," and in the acceptance of the subordination of women to men and of all Christians to their bishop.

The conflict within the Spanish church reflected in the *Acts of the Council of Saragossa* was not, then, so much a conflict between ascetics and an anti-ascetic episcopacy as a conflict between two different emerging understandings of Christian asceticism and, correspondingly, of Christian authority. Transposing the terminology of the Egyptian desert to the context of the Spanish town, we might describe it more specifically as a conflict between "eremitism" and "cenobitism." In this case, the conflict was particularly acute precisely because neither party withdrew to the seclusion of monastery or wilderness but both remained firmly rooted in the urban community.

Ambrose and Martin and the Two Asceticisms

The council of Saragossa did not immediately resolve the conflict in the Spanish churches. In fact, it is clear from the writings of Priscillian and Sulpicius Severus that the rift between the two parties deepened in the years following. In the course of the series of disputes which have come to be known as the "Priscillianist controversy," a number of well-known figures in the Christian West were forced to take sides or express opinions. The positions of Martin of Tours and Ambrose of Milan are particularly instructive. While Martin expressed some sympathy for Priscillian and the other ascetics opposed by the bishops at Saragossa and later at Trier, Ambrose sided with the Saragossan bishops. Their positions in the controversy correspond, I suggest, to their respective understandings of Christian discipline and authority. And it is Ambrose, more even than Severus' monk-bishop Martin, who exemplifies the deep influence of cenobitic asceticism on the Western episcopacy.

Martin intervened twice on behalf of the Spanish ascetics—though he did not, according to Severus, deny that at least some of them had fallen into heresy. When an episcopal council meeting at Bordeaux had turned over the judgment of Priscillian and his Spanish and Gallic companions to the emperor Maximus, Martin vigorously petitioned both Maximus and bishop Ithacius not to bring Priscillian to a civil trial in which blood might be shed.

> He said that it was enough and more than enough that, judged heretical by episcopal decision, they should be thrown out of the churches.... (Severus, *Chronicle* 2.50).

Ithacius, a Spanish bishop of the Saragossan party and Priscillian's chief accuser, turned a deaf ear to Martin's requests. Severus charges Ithacius with being "excessively devoted to the pleasures of sensuality," and protests that

> his foolishness went so far that all—even holy men—who possessed a zeal for reading or were determined to struggle by fasting he labelled associates or disciples of Priscillian (*Chronicle* 2.50).

Martin himself was among those ascetics whom Ithacius charged with heresy. When Martin eventually left Trier, Priscillian was, as he had feared, tried and sentenced to death. Martin subsequently returned to the imperial court upon learning that Maximus planned to send tribunes into Spain to seek out still more "heretics" and deprive them of their lives or property. Martin suspected that such a witch-hunt would end in the destruction not only of "heretics" but also of many whom he considered truly holy and ascetic.

> For at that time judgments were based on appearances alone, since one was considered a heretic on account of pallor or dress rather than faith (Severus, *Dialogues* 3.11).

Moreover, Martin desired to protect even those whom he (or at least Severus) acknowledged to be "heretics" or followers of Priscillian.

Martin's sympathy for Priscillian and the other Spanish ascetics is not surprising when one considers that he seems to have shared with those Spaniards an emphasis on the study of scripture and fasting and— broadly speaking—the cultivation of a personal discipline from which his exceptional authority derived. Severus strives, on one level, to present Martin as first and foremost a bishop and an example to bishops; in his *Dialogues* he even states that he is not going to talk about the period before Martin's episcopacy (1.27). However, his writings in fact depict Martin primarily as a hermit and freelance miracle-worker, and it is easy at times to forget Martin's episcopal identity. The "authority" which so overwhelms Severus when he is in Martin's presence (*Life of Martin* 25) is not the authority of episcopal office but the authority of the saint; this is made explicit when Severus comments that Martin's authority was diminished when he became bishop (*Dialogues* 2.4) and when he had dealings with other bishops (*Dialogues* 3.13). Martin, moreover, faces serious opposition from other bishops (*Life* 27; *Dialogues* 1.2, 1.26). Severus gives us practically no information about the bishop's relationship with his own congregation at Tours and relates that Martin lived outside the city "in the solitude of a hermit" (*Life* 10). He was in fact surrounded by some eighty disciples, but even in this monastic context, he is depicted more as an exemplary anchorite than as a cenobitic monk.

Ambrose's response to the Priscillianist controversy as well as his understanding of asceticism and the episcopacy contrast markedly with Martin's. Shortly after the Council of Saragossa, both sides in the Spanish conflict appealed to the bishop of Milan for support. Hydatius of Merida, one of the Saragossan bishops, wrote to Ambrose accusing Priscillian and two other ascetic bishops of Manicheism (Priscillian, *Tractate* 2.41). Soon thereafter, Priscillian and the two other bishops were exiled and journeyed to Milan to appeal to Ambrose in person (Priscillian, *Tractate* 2.41; Severus, *Chronicle* 2.48). They met with rebuff, and it is likely that Ambrose had been at least partly responsible for Gratian's issuance of the rescript against "Manichees and pseudo-bishops" on the basis of which the Spanish ascetics had been exiled in the first place (*Tractate* 2.40; *Chronicle* 2.47). Ambrose was later to find himself in Trier near the end of Priscillian's trial. He refused communion with the bishops seeking the Priscillianists' death and lamented the cruel treatment of one aged supporter of Priscillian (*Letter* 24.12). However, his action appears to have been deliberately calculated to alienate Maximus for reasons extraneous to the Priscillianist controversy, and his opposition to Priscillian's persecutors was limited to a denunciation of the participation of bishops in civil trials involving capital punishment.

Ambrose's position in the Priscillianist controversy seems, like Martin's, to reflect his understanding of Christian discipline and authority, and here he found himself in close agreement with the Council of Saragossa, if not with the process at Trier. For Ambrose, the monastery was not only a training ground for an episcopal elite, as it was for Severus and Martin, but also a model for the bishop's congregation. The urban congregation, placed in sharp juxtaposition to the sinful "world" which surrounded it, became the arena of a lifestyle of communal discipline and self-denial. While the female virgin most aptly symbolized for Ambrose the sacred integrity of the community (Brown: 341-365), the bishop unquestionably provided the focus of authority. Explicit parallels between Ambrose and the Saragossan council occur in the area of liturgical innovation. Like the bishops of Saragossa, Ambrose advocated a life of common worship focused on the episcopally led community. He urged the Christians of Milan to attend daily services at the cathedral at sunrise and sunset, as well as occasional public vigils; he composed hymns to be sung at the daily services (Taft: 141–143, 174–176). Ambrose's biographer goes so far as to credit the bishop with the introduction of the daily offices and vigils to the western churches:

> [During the course of the conflict with the Arians over the basilica] antiphons, hymns, and vigils first began to be practiced in the Milanese church. The devotion to this practice continues even today not only in the same church but through almost all the provinces of the West. (Paulinus of Milan, *Life of Ambrose* 13; cf. Augustine, *Confessions* 9.7).

In Ambrose, we glimpse the emergence of an integrated understanding of an ascetic episcopacy in which the tension between the roles of ascetic and bishop experienced by figures like Martin and his biographer Severus is virtually non-existent.

Conclusions: The Conciliar Text and the Cenobitic Bishop

Philip Rousseau has illustrated the significant role played by hagiographic biography in forging the link between "ascetic authority in the desert" and "episcopal authority in Gaul" (5). At the center of this literary tradition stands Sulpicius Severus' *Life of Martin*, which represents a crucial stage "in the process whereby sanctity was harnessed to the purposes of the church" through the merging of episcopal and ascetic authority in the exemplary figure of the bishop of Tours (165). I have here argued that conciliar documents like the *Acts of the Council of Saragossa* have a place alongside hagiographic works like Sulpicius Severus' *Life of Martin* or Paulinus' *Life of Ambrose* in the evolution of an ascetic—or, more precisely, cenobitic—episcopacy. Indeed, whereas the *Life of Martin* betrays many signs of tension between the essentially eremitic authority of the holy Martin and his authority as bishop, the *Acts of the Council of Saragossa* reflect a cenobitic discipline which is more intimately and harmoniously united with the authority of the episcopacy. While opposing individualistically oriented ascetic practices, the *Acts* advocate a model of Christian lifestyle focused on the corporate worship of the urban congregation and strict obedience to the norms of the community as taught and exemplified by its bishop.

The "asceticism" of the *Acts of the Council of Saragossa* is a product not only of its content but also, I suggest, of its form. Geoffrey Harpham has proposed that "narrative is virtually the ascetical form of discourse" (45), arguing that temptation is central to both asceticism and narrative (67). The conciliar text can also be viewed as an "ascetical form of discourse," albeit a much more limited form than narrative. In the *Acts,* the images of the potential transgressors of the proposed discipline are vividly evoked, while at the same time a voice of authority urges—indeed, seems to expect—not transgression but obedience. Breaking off in the dramatic moment of the episcopal pronouncement, the text leaves the reader's response to temptation open and unresolved, thereby calling attention to the desire to transgress while exhorting resistance to that desire. The form of the *Acts of the Council of Saragossa* thus echoes its content, giving shape to an evolving "asceticism" of obedience to episcopal authority and to the norms of the episcopally led community.

WORKS CONSULTED

Brown, Peter.
    1988   *The Body and Society: Men, Women, and Sexual Renunciation in Early Christianity.* New York: Columbia University Press.

Chadwick, Henry.
    1976   *Priscillian of Avila: The Occult and the Charismatic in the Early Church.* Oxford: Clarendon.

Dudden, F. Homes.
    1935   *The Life and Times of St. Ambrose.* Oxford: Clarendon.

Harpham, Geoffrey Galt.
    1987   *The Ascetic Imperative in Culture and Criticism.* Chicago: University of Chicago Press.

Hess, Hamilton.
    1958   *The Canons of the Council of Sardica, A.D. 343.* Oxford: Clarendon.

Leuchli, Samuel.
    1972   *Power and Sexuality: The Emergence of Canon Law at the Synod of Elvira.* Philadelphia: Temple University Press.

Primero Concilio Caesaraugustano. MDC Aniversario.
    1981   Zaragoza.

Ramos y Loscertales, José María.
    1952   *Prisciliano. Gesta rerum.* Universidad de Salamanca.

Rousseau, Philip.
   1978   *Ascetics, Authority, and the Church in the Age of Jerome and Cassian*. Oxford: Oxford University Press.

Stancliffe, Claire.
   1983   *St. Martin and His Hagiographer: History and Miracle in Sulpicius Severus*. Oxford: Clarendon.

Taft, Robert.
   1986   *The Liturgy of the Hours in East and West*. Collegeville, MN: The Liturgical Press.

Vollman, Benedikt.
   1974   "Priscillianus." *PW* suppl. 14. Cols. 485–559.

A REGIMEN FOR SALVATION
MEDICAL MODELS IN MANICHAEAN ASCETICISM

Jason David BeDuhn
Indiana University

ABSTRACT

In Manichaeism, salvation for the individual ascetic begins with a realignment and rectification of physiological processes, which is described in the contemporary language of medicine. Did the Manichaeans use this medical language metaphorically or literally? This paper demonstrates the literal character of Manichaean ascetical language as part of an analysis of the relationship between discourse and practice in Manichaeism. After a discussion of the propensity among scholars to metaphorize religious discourse, I present material from both Manichaeism (*CMC*, *Kephalaia*, and the *Ruwanagan* ritual) and the contemporaneous Hellenistic medical discipline. From these materials, I show the permeability of discourses usually thought of as distinct, and the direct engagement of Manichaean "religious" discourse with medical concerns and concepts. Ascetic practice among the Manichaeans is shown to involve a regimen of controlling and manipulating the body for salvational ends. This practice is grounded in a direct, *literal* apprehension of human physiology which, if metaphorized, could not function in that role. We must be careful, therefore, in our analysis of "religious" discourse, and not be too quick to metaphorize utterances which seem "inappropriate" to it. Ascetic practice constructs its own "reality" in relation to its motivating discourse, and it is not unnatural that this "reality" focuses, in quite *concrete* terms, on the body.

The function of the language of asceticism is to induce ascetic behavior in those who participate in its matrix of discourse. The discourse cannot be understood as an end in itself, but must be examined in light of the praxis which it seeks to institute and legitimate.[1] In asceticism, discourse and practice are involved in a mutual construction in which both are essential factors, and in which neither can long survive the absence of the other.[2] Ascetic statements can generate ascetic behavior in those receptive to it; ascetic practice also generates appropriate statements, characterizations, and perspectives which reinforce the practice. Because of their motivational function, these statements persist, and interact as a discourse, even when they are at odds with the broader religious "tradition" in which the ascetic practice situates itself.[3] The discourse and practice of asceticism together produce a reality of their own, with its own built-in perspectives and motivations.

Motivation can be produced rhetorically by a number of different strategies of discourse. These strategies include analogy, metaphor, hyperbole and similar modes of discourse in which one recognizes and utilizes a disjunction between statement and perception in a creative way. These strategies exist side by side with more direct modes of discourse which claim to represent "reality" exactly as it is, albeit through the medium of language.[4] Anthropologists and other scholars have long pondered the issues of "belief" and "metaphor" in relation to the world-views which institute and legitimate the structures of particular cultures. When they encounter a religious tradition which institutes an apprehension of the world at odds with scientific knowledge, the western champions of that "scientific" perspective have felt compelled to determine the relative literal or metaphorical "meaning" of its statements for those who both generate them and are in turn constructed by them.[5]

Western scholars' ascription of meaning to statements made by others is in large part determined by the discourse in which these statements are perceived to engage. Thus the translation and interpretation of key terms will vary with respect to whether a text is considered to be, for example, medical, philosophical, or religious. This is not in itself incorrect; in fact, due regard for discursive context is essential for a reasonable reading of any text.[6] But the assignment of texts to particular discourses, and the resultant judgments of literal or metaphorical meaning, may reflect a much more insidious agenda than first appearances would seem to indicate. In the final analysis, this interpretive process generates decisions about what is "appropriate" to a given discourse, and sets up a normative hermeneutic that treats as "metaphor" any language which resists conventional discursive expectations.

I will begin where these issues began for me: with a Greek text from the fifth Century which we call the *Cologne Mani Codex* (hereafter CMC). In CMC 80.22 to 82.23, Mani criticizes the baptismal purifications of the Elchasaites.

> [This] washing by which you wash your food (Mani says) is of [no avail]. For this body is defiled and molded from a mold of defilement [*plaseōs miarotētos*]. You can see how, whenever someone cleanses his food and partakes of that which has just been washed, it is apparent to us that from it still come blood [*haima*] and bile [*cholē*] and gases [*pneumata*] and shameful excrements [*skubala*] and bodily defilement [*miarotēs*]. But if someone were to keep his mouth away from this food for a few days, immediately all these excretions [*apekdumata*] of shame and loathsomeness will be found to be lacking and wanting [in the] body. But if [that one] were to partake [again] of [food, in the] same way they would again abound in the body, so that it is manifest that they flow out [*plēmmurousin*] from the food itself. Now if someone else were to partake of food [which is] washed and cleansed, and partake (also) of that which is unwashed, it is clear that the wellness [*kallos*] and the strength [*dunamis*] of the body is recognizably the same. Likewise, the loathsomeness

and dregs [*trux*] of both are seen not to differ from each other, so that what has been washed—which [it (i.e., the body) rejected] and sloughed off [*ape(rripse k)ai exedusato*]—is not at all distinguishable from that [other] which is unwashed.

And a little further along in this speech Mani concludes:

> Therefore, [make an inspection of] yourselves as to [what] your purity [*katha(rotēs)*] [really is. For it is] impossible to purify [*katharisai*] your bodies entirely—for each day the body is disturbed [*kineitai*] and comes to rest [*histatai*] through the secretions [*ekkriseis*] of sediments [*hupostathmēs*] from it—so that the action comes about without a commandment of the Savior [*hōs kai genesthai to pragma dicha entolēs tēs tou sōtēros*]. The purity [*katharotēs*], then, which was spoken about, is that which comes through knowledge, separation of light from darkness and of death from life and of living waters from turbid [*tethambōmenon*], so that [you] may know [that] each is [. . .] one another and [. . .] the commandments of the Savior, [so that . . .] might redeem the soul [*psuchē*] from [annihilation] and destruction. This is in truth the genuine purity . . . (CMC 83.20–85.3).

Had they survived as isolated fragments—heavily laced as they are with medical terminology,[7] arguing as they do on the basis of demonstrations and proofs, treating of issues of biology and pathology—these passages might have been assigned to a medical treatise. Only the mention of a Savior adds a dimension of religiosity, and suggests that something more is going on here. But what exactly is going on? If this is a medical text, why the appeal to a Savior? If this is a religious text, why is it so immersed in medical language and concerns? We have here, it seems, a discursive dilemma.

Modern western scholars delineate discourses based largely on analogy with contemporary discursive boundaries which have little or no correspondence with those of historically or culturally distinct populations, and which are not nearly as solid and clear even in our own culture as we like to believe (Foucault, 1972: 22). After this ethnocentric determination, judgments of literal or metaphoric interpretation are made based upon it. Thus the statements of a medical text will be treated as literal, and the larger discourse on medicine is considered a literal treatment of the various objects and concepts involved.[8] Statements in a religious text, or which are part of a religious discourse, on the other hand, are thought to engage different objects, enunciative modalities, concepts and strategies from those found in the medical or philosophical discourses, and therefore are treated differently—i.e. with a much greater propensity for metaphorization. It is for this reason that the history of science and the history of religions are such different enterprises, and employ such different languages of evaluation. The history of science judges statements of the past and of other cultures as "right" or "wrong," as "dead-ends" or as "key developments," the *telos* of which is always the modern western apprehension of the universe. The history of religions seeks to avoid such judgments, to eliminate appraisal by the measure of our own cultural ideologies. But in order to abandon forever the formerly common characterization of other cultures as ignorant, superstitious, and unsophisticated, we have introduced a new form of ideological imperialism.[9]

Through interpretation, we seek to be "generous" to the culturally Other, removing his or her statements from the realm of an objective reality where we would regard them as incorrect or deficient (the history of science model) to a domain of metaphor, symbolism, and poetry where statements are not about reality but affect (the history of religions model). Therefore,

> ... the urge to see 'metaphors' is ... ethnocentric insofar as it assimilates other peoples' 'facts' to our idea of 'meaningful fiction' (Sandor: 101–2).
>
> To regard other people's direct predications, including their myths, as metaphorical means that one does not believe in the facts of the manifest content ... and yet would like to give the predications meaning, *and meaning only*, by making use of the manifest content. To think of metaphors means to rescue the belief in meaning, not the belief in things (114).

Despite its claim for cultural relativism, such an approach amounts to the very opposite; it glosses the differences between cultures, and presupposes shared categories of meaning and common discursive formations.[10]

Just how illegitimate this attitude is becomes clear when we take in hand texts such as the one under discussion. If we can forego an almost automatic, culturally prejudiced, judgment of what this text is for us, indeed what it must be, given our apprehension of reality, we can take up the question of what this text was for those who composed, copied, read and used it in conjunction with their ascetic practice. We can determine its metaphoric or literal status from other significant statements of and about the Manichaeans, coupled with the known details of their ritual ascetic practices. Roger Keesing, who wants to warn against the opposite problem—of taking the conventional metaphor of others out of context and treating it literally when its own employers do not—suggests that "our safeguards against spuriously imputing metaphysical beliefs to our subjects, which appear to be implied by their ways of talk, principally consist of skepticism and a *relentless search for supporting evidence outside the realm of language*" (212, emphasis added). In this paper, I use Manichaean ritual action as such non-linguistic evidence. It becomes clear from both the linguistic and non-linguistic source material that not only this text but Manichaeism as a whole defies our neatly crafted delineations of discursive fields and shows us a place where the distinct discourses familiar to us become permeable, overlapped, integrated, and redefined.[11]

In taking up the question of whether Manichaean statements relating to ascetic practice are literal or metaphorical, I am not concerned with the rediscovery, behind the given population of events and statements, of intention, consciousness, or meaning. As part of an analysis of discursive formations, the question of literality and metaphoricity involves the *relations* among the apparent statements and events themselves—i.e. whether Manichaean discourse on asceticism and salvation has a direct or mediated relation to Manichaean ascetic practices.

Manichaean texts describe light and darkness, good and evil, as two totally alien *material* substances whose cataclysmic mixture has brought about the current state of our existence. Before one attains to the Manichaean understanding of the universe and its associated ascetic practice, it is said, the pure elements of the body are subject to the conditions produced by the primordial conflict and subsequent mixture. Hence the pure elements are bound to a putrifying construct of flesh and blood and hunger and gases (*Kephalaion* 94: 239.10–30).[12] Each of these defiling substances emits into the body pollutants which disturb the human being. Thus blood emits anger (*blke*) which in turn causes rheumatism. Hunger emits gall (*sishe*) which in turn causes fever. Flesh emits a gloomy vapor (*ōkme*) which in turn causes impudence. Gases emit some nefarious substance (lost in a lacunae) which in turn causes tears. All together these comprise the twelve pollutants of the body, fed by the intake of food.

But upon accepting Manichaeism and its discipline of holiness, the believer's body is recast as a New Being, ruled by the mind of light. The pure elements are released from their entrapment in defiling bodily substances. The body is purified by the strict asceticism of the elect, and reaches a perfected and efficient state through which the pure elements contained in food may be released from their own corruption in the *oikonomia* of the "soul-meal" (*trophē npsuchikos*) (*Kephalaion* 94: 240.1–9). This function of the body was an imperative of salvation, expected from the Manichaean ascetic elect and performed daily in their ritual feeding, called in Iranian texts the *Ruwanagan*.[13]

The *Ruwanagan* ritual was the focus of the Manichaean support network, and was the sole recipient of food-alms from Manichaean adherents. Reduced to its basic features, the ritual proceeded as follows: After sundown, the adherents of the religion would present fruit, vegetables and bread along with fruit juices to the assembled elect. The latter would bless the contributors and relieve them from the sin of having harmed living things in the procurement of food (Augustine, *De Haeresibus*, 46, 118–127). The elect would also make a formal apology to the food itself for the ordeal of its harvest, preparation, and digestion (*Acta Archelai*, 10: 16f.; Cyril of Jerusalem, *Catechesis* VI, 32; Anonymous, *Epistle Against the*

Manichaeans[14]). But the tribulation of the life in food on its way to (and through) the elect resulted in liberation from the condition of mixture, and it is said that Manichaean adherents looked forward to reincarnation as plants so that they might more quickly reach the celestial paradise through the bowels of the elect.[15]

The elect, for their part, were expected to meditate on the function and implication of the meal and its relation to the central Manichaean myth of primordial strife and mixture (Henning: 41). The food was identified as the very substance of the Manichaean God, which the elect took into their bodies, not to divinize themselves, but so that their bodies could serve as the purifying mechanism of liberation (Augustine, *Contra Faustum*, 2.5). Under all these conditions, the ritual proceeded with the consumption of the food by the elect, whose adherence to a strict ascetic regimen entailed this being their only meal of the day. The performance of the ritual then continued in an internal sacred space, by means of the apparatus of each elect's digestive system.

In the stomach and intestinal tract, the heat of hunger—an evil force domesticated by the elect to the service of salvation (Chavannes and Pelliot: 537–39)—rendered the food into its constituent substances. For the Manichaeans, of course, these substances were reducible to two: the good and the evil, or—to speak in appropriately physiological terms—nutriment and excrement. The good material flowed out of the digestive system and through the five anatomical substances—bone, vein, nerve, flesh and skin—from which it was thought to emanate in various fashions and ultimately make its way to the celestial paradise (Ephrem Syrus, *2nd Discourse*, 31 and 43).[16] The evil material was reduced and compacted into waste products and evacuated from the body. As summed up in *Kephalaion* 79:

> [The] soul [*psychē*] which comes into [the body] by means of the *oikonomia* of [the body's] food [*trophē*] day by day, is refined and purified [by fasting] and is cleansed from mixture [*synkrasis*] [with] the darkness....[17]

All of this additional information reflects back upon our first text and builds resistance to our metaphorizing interpretive tendencies—our inclination to treat physical language as metaphorical when it appears in a "religious" text. Are we to take these central practices of Manichaean life as enacted metaphors for some spiritual truth?[18] Not a single shred of evidence lends itself to such an interpretation. All of the testimony available to us—from the Manichaeans themselves, from their observers, and from their enemies—is in full agreement that the *Ruwanagan* ritual, the key activity of daily Manichaean practice, was believed to function literally, exactly as presented, as a physiological resolution of an existential conflict. The *Ruwanagan*, its prerequisite ascetic practice, and the discourse on metabolic salvation with which they were engaged, display a set of relations with the contemporary ancient discipline of medicine and language of physiology which may force us to reconsider the boundaries of ancient discourse.[19] It is not a question of a practice being informed by more than one discourse, but rather the interpenetration of discourses through their common engagement with a practice.

If we are surprised by this permeability and interaction of fields of discourse normally treated as unrelated, it is because our own cultural delineations of discourse have led us to view salvation in a spiritualized, non-physical light, as a set of concepts and concerns totally contained within the "religious" discourse in which any incongruous terminology and expression is treated as metaphor. The reading-back of our own "spiritual" categories into Manichaeism is precisely the point at issue. At stake is more than one text or one ritual but the whole nature of Manichaean dualism, which, in the face of all evidence to the contrary, has been consistently Hellenized, Platonized,[20] and Christianized into a spirit/matter opposition by its non-Manichaean interpreters. The gross physicality of the Manichaean "soul-stuff," and even the Manichaean deity, has been invariably metaphorized by modern scholars habituated to the rules of "religious" discourse.

This metaphorizing hermeneutic is so pervasive that it would be pointless for me to cite individual examples. Very few among those who have taken up the study of Manichaeism have managed to avoid it. Many of these scholars know better, and state quite clearly the literal, physical, direct character of Manichaean discourse. Yet they lapse back into the habits of language in which their scholarship is imbedded and return to the simplifying dualities of our own culture, inadvertently demonstrating the world-constructing power of the discourses we inhabit. The problem in endemic not only to Manichaean studies, but to the study of religion in general. It has been the very nature of our field to "interpret" the utterances of our subjects in order to find *behind* those utterances "what they mean." We debate strongly among ourselves *how* to interpret, how to find the "meaning" of religious utterances, but we do not question the interpretive strategy itself. That strategy is a given, imbedded in the academic discourse we inhabit, and our adherence to it is the price we pay for our place of authority within the discourse.

Manichaean ascetic practice developed in a world whose discourse on health and well-being was quite different from our own and involved different sets of objects, concepts, modes of enunciation, and strategies of relation. We can see in this "medical" discourse a greater degree of permeability than we have been led to expect from our culture's own discourse on health. Once we recognize the set of relations which defines the ancient Hellenistic discourse on health and sets it apart from our own, we can also see that Manichaean statements concerning the body, health, and ascetic practice are engaged in this discourse and grounded upon it.

The period of history and the cultural sphere in which Manichaeism originated and flourished is full of examples of discursive permeability between the spheres of philosophy, medicine, and religion, between the professions of sophist, scientist, physician and prophet. Figures of authority commonly propounded regimens of life which were intended as modes of "salvation" from human misery, and each sought to root their regimen in the inherent structures of the universe.[21] Mani was one of these figures. Formulator of an elaborate and comprehensive "religious" apprehension of the world, he first introduced himself to the Persian shah Shapur as "a doctor from Babylon" (M556).[22] He exorcised demons, issued dietetic instruction, and was known even to his enemies as a physician—although, as they said, not a very good one.[23]

Perhaps the most important corollary of such discursive permeability is that the concerns of what we call the human "soul" were considered fully a part of science and medicine, as well as religion (Frede: 227). To the vast majority of physicians, scientists, and philosophers active in the Hellenistic arena, the human soul—regardless of its ultimate origin or nature --subsisted in the human body as a vapor produced and maintained by metabolic processes.[24] According to the Stoic Chrysippus, "each soul is a bit of unified *pneuma*, and all psychic phenomena—including the passions and emotions—are states of this *pneuma* . . ." (Gould: 159; cf. Edelstein: 355; Temkin: 159; Brock, 1929: 235). "For the Stoics," Fritz Steckerl explains, "the passions were diseases" (Steckerl: 43).[25]

Nemesius of Emesa (late fourth Century), in his survey of the different philosophical, scientific and medical views of the soul found in the "ancient authors," contrasts corporealists to incorporealists, pluralists (who believe in multiple souls) to monists (who believe in a common soul-substance), substantialists to "harmonists" (who think the soul is just a balanced mixture of elements) (Telfer: 257–272). Nemesius discusses the Manichaeans in this context: they believe "that one and the same universal soul is parcelled out to the several animate beings, and will return to exist by itself again" (259–60). The materialistic aspects of this view are elaborated later:

> . . . ensouled beings receive more [soul-substance], and . . . inanimates receive less, while much the most part resides in heaven . . . they assert that the soul-substance is divided up. And the worst thing of all is that they would have us believe the soul-substance to be literally mingled with the elements, and that, when bodies are generated, the portion of soul for them is separated off,

together with those elements... parcelling out its substance, representing it as corporeal, and subjecting it to passions (286).

Anonymous Londinensis, perhaps the single most valuable record of Hellenistic medical theory, begins with a discussion of the relation of psychic states to physical ones, and testifies to a long and widespread tradition which viewed what we call the soul as a physiological product subject to metabolic effects (Jones).[26] Galen argues that "when we produce by means of food and drink and by our daily activities a good bodily temperament (*eucrasia*), we thereby also influence the soul (*psychē*) towards goodness" (Brock, 1929: 233). He opposes the incorporeal views of the Middle Platonists with a litany of digestive processes (240). In Philo, the Therapeutae are said to

> ... profess an art of healing better than that current in the cities which cures only bodies, while theirs treats also souls oppressed with grievous and well nigh incurable diseases, inflicted by pleasures [*hēdonai*] and desires [*epithumiai*] and griefs [*lupai*] and fears [*phoboi*] [as well as by] acts of covetousness, folly and injustice, and the excess [*plēthos*] of the other passions and vices ... (*The Contemplative Life*, 2; *cf. Kephalaion* 86).

Note that Philo sums up this list of disturbances of psychic health as *plēthos*, that is, excesses; exactly the same word is employed in medical texts to describe the production of pollutants by digestion (Jones: 33–59; Vallance: 126–29). This idea of a flux of pollutants arising from defective digestion—found throughout Near Eastern and Mediterranean medicine and traceable to Egyptian antecedents (Saunders: 22)—is shared by Mani, and, as we have seen, is discussed by him in the *Cologne Mani Codex* and in the *Kephalaia*.

Such correlation of human metabolism and spirit, and concern with their interaction, depend upon physiological systems such as those expressed by Praxagoras of Cos or Asclepiades of Bithynia, and the Manichaean physiological system is analogous to them not only in structure, but also in many points of detail. Praxagoras constructed a unified anatomical theory which considered the human body to be permeated by ever finer channels which carry first *chulē*, then blood, then the gaseous material (the "soul") which drives the human motor system (Steckerl). The conscious, motive self, or soul, was considered an *anathumiasis* (vaporous exhalation) of the blood (44). For Asclepiades of Bithynia, the *psychē* is made entirely of *pneuma*, which in turn consists of "light, round lumps which are frail" (Vallance: 22–23). In the medical system of Praxagoras, "normal, healthy digestion is characterized by the formation of blood" (Steckerl: 10–11). "The rising of bubbles (in the blood) is a normal feature of digestion. The production of air included in these bubbles is a continuous physiological process which accompanies the transformation of food into blood" (20). The bubbles flow in the blood, through the veins and into the arteries, where the pulse collapses the bubbles, releasing the *pneuma* in them. The arteries, now full of *pneuma*, ramify into the nerves and sinews—which were widely thought to be identical in this time (Brock, 1929: 125–29), a view reflected in the Manichaean anatomical system. The *pneuma* operates in the nerves and sinews as the carrier of intention and voluntary movement to the body (Phillips: 25). This, too, is clearly paralleled in Manichaean literature.[27] Under normal conditions, the harmful byproducts of food are evacuated from the body, but an excess or deficiency of digestive heat disrupts the digestive process and produces a flux of harmful humors which invade the body and cause illness—both physical and psychic (Steckerl: 82–83).

The view that maintenance of the proper degree of digestive heat was crucial to health was widely shared. The Hippocratic work *Breaths* states that cold gases (*physai*) percolating up from a defective digestion have a chilling effect on blood flow (7): such pathogenic vapors constitute "the most active agents during all diseases" (15)[28] and are responsible for the abundance of life-threatening fevers. Phylotimus of Cos advises against drinking cold water with a meal (Steckerl: 116), and to this Galen adds the taking of cold baths (71): both were felt to suppress digestion and constrict the arteries by the production of cold phlegm. Compare with these statements from "medical" discourse the heretofore puzzling testimony that bathing was forbidden to the Manichaean elect on the grounds that it "freezes the soul" (*Acta Archelai*, 10), or the caricature by Ephrem Syrus that cold phlegm is "the great enemy of the school of Mani" (*2nd Discourse*, 42).[29]

Greek physiological systems commonly assumed an outflow of metabolic end-products from the body, e.g. Galen's concept of *ekptosis* (Siegel, 1970:77; 1973:94; May: 55–56; Steuer and Saunders: 57). Nemesius of Emesa tells us that "a living creature keeps passing off matter, through the visible orifices, and through others that are concealed as well. . . . Whatever is evacuated must, of course, be fully replaced, or the living organism would perish from the deficiency of replacements" (Telfer: 240–41). Asclepiades of Bithynia "explained disorders by appealing to a blockage of corpuscles which in the healthy body percolate through invisible pores in the body" (Vallance: 15). He claimed that "there are continuous emanations from us to the outside world, which vary according to the prevailing condition" (Sextus Empiricus, *Adversus mathematicos* 3.5). This "natural conveyance of corpuscles out of the body" is so strong that "the force of their exit inhibits cicatrization" of wounds (Vallance: 105, quoting Cassius the Iatrosophist). Manichaean physiology requires similar pathways of exudation in order to transport the light liberated by metabolism to the heavens (M363; *Kephalaion* 86).

For all this aetiological comparability, one might still object that a "religious" tradition such as Manichaeism lacks the accoutrements of a medical practice. But the general view in the historical and cultural milieu with which we are concerned, and one easily forgotten in our age of drugs and surgery, was "that medicine was, in essentials, merely a branch ... of the science of dietetics" (Jones: 158).[30] And once we enter the arena of dietetics we are in a world not only of food and nutrition, but also of purities and impurities, taboos and cuisines, discourses of identity, ethics, and cosmology—in short, a domain where discursive distinctions break down and reconstruct themselves.[31] It is not my intent to argue for Manichaean familiarity with any particular school or text of Hellenistic medicine. I propose instead that these schools and texts share themes and bodies of knowledge which permeated the medical "discipline" of the time, and that each school or text—including the Manichaeans—builds upon these shared bases of discourse.[32] Mani and his successors were involved in this dialogue, and the practices and theories of Manichaean asceticism presuppose this discourse.

Manichaean physiology does appear unique in at least one respect, in that defective digestion and the production of bodily pollutants is considered to be an inherent pathological condition, rather than a temporary imbalance. As the broader Manichaean mythology makes clear, this is a congenital corruption, and its destructive effects arise in the digestive system automatically, in the given condition of human existence (i.e., *genesthai ... dicha entolēs tēs tou sōtēros* [CMC 83.20ff.]).[33] Apart from the commandments of the Savior—that is, the Manichaean regimen—digestion can only have negative and disturbing results.[34] But contrasted with this pathological condition, both in the CMC and elsewhere, is the possibility of redeeming the "soul" (*psychē*)—both one's own luminous nature and that found in food—through adherence to the Manichaean regimen which involves the knowledge of the secret of separation.[35] Salvation was, by this account, dependent upon the ability of the elect to "succeed in digesting their dinner," as Augustine laconically puts it (*Contra Faustum*, 2.5). The Manichaean physiological scheme maintains an attenuated thematic relation to Galen's view that "the digestion of food in the stomach involves a *metabolē* of it into the quality proper to that which is receiving nourishment" (*On the Natural Faculties*, 241).[36] In Manichaean discourse, "that which is receiving nourishment" is the luminous "soul-stuff" and ultimately the heavenly realm of light. But the successful metabolism of God/light/soul-material could only be achieved by surmounting the inherent resistances of bodily malfunction (see Foucault, 1977a: 29–30).

The victorious ascendancy of light in the individual believer is not, however, an irreversible transformation of the body. Enrollment in the Manichaean program of salvation is neither a Christian redemption nor a Gnostic liberation, but more on the order of a dietetic regimen. The elect were never considered unassailably pure; and the adherents, who constituted the all-important support network for the elect, were instructed to certify the sanctity of the lifestyle of an elect before offering any *Ruwanagan* alms (*Xuastvanift; Compendium*). The elect practitioner who failed to adhere to the strict ascetic regimen to which he or she was sworn would be deprived of food, and hence would face the unpleasant choice of penance, abandonment of the faith, or starvation. In this way, the Manichaean authorities crafted a tight network of interdependence and a set of checks on adherence to the regimen.

The disciplined life imposed on the elect was based upon a conceptualization of the channels through which the *pneumatic* end-products of digestive purification were thought to flow. These channels are set forth for us in *Kephalaion* 104 ("On Food [*trophē*]: that it determines the five products [*jpo*, lit.: 'births'] in the human body").

> This food [*trophē*] which people gather in in various kinds, when they eat it [and] it comes into the body, it disseminates to the five products. The first product is that which comes out of the person in meditation, and it rises up in the mind [*nous*], and it comes out in all his limbs without measure. The second is that which comes out of the person in voice and speech. The third is that which vibrates [*bachf*] in strength and vigor. The fourth is that which is born in the lust [*hēdonē*] of desire [*epithumia*] between men and women. The fifth is that which is formed and is fashioned in the flesh, and is born and comes out—which is bodily birth. . . .

In response to these natural channels, which could potentially thrust refined light or *pneuma* back into the mixture of the world, Mani imposed the five-fold rest, or *anapausis*, which was the precondition for the status of elect and participation in the *Ruwanagan*. The five rests are:

1. Truthfulness: the rest of the mind (*nous*)
2. Dietary asceticism: the rest of the mouth[37]
3. Non-injury: the rest of the hands
4. Chastity: the rest from desire
5. Poverty: the rest from wordly concern.

By these disciplines, the Manichaean elect effectively blocked the detrimental channels of *pneumatic* emanation: the vow of poverty precluded the production of offspring who were considered a burdensome and mundane involvement as well as a reentrapment of life;[38] the vow of chastity eliminated the exudation of lustful energies; non-injury entailed the cessation of all harmful action and, indeed, the expending of energies in labor of any kind. But in the case of the two remaining rests (those of the mind and mouth) the goal was purification rather than elimination. In this way, these two channels could still serve as pathways for the flow of liberated soul-stuff, the victorious light, which departed from the body and proceeded to the celestial paradise (see figure). Indeed, Augustine and Ephrem specifically refer to meditations, prayers and psalms as the activity appropriate to the elect and associated with the liberating activity of the *Ruwanagan* (Augustine, *Morals of the Manichaeans*, 36; Ephrem Syrus, *1st Discourse*, 27).

The reparation, then, of the inherent pathology of the body and the maintenance of digestive salvation was dependent upon a regimen of life within the same discourse of concern as those imposed by other prophets, physicians and philosophers of the ancient world; these regimens were intended for the health of the individual—body and soul—and for the salvation of the individual from the condition of human suffering in all its manifestations.[39] What distinguishes Manichaeism from strictly medical models of human well-being in this comparative context is the employment of the purified and reordered human body as a mechanism of purification for the entire universe and, ultimately, for God itself. But the engagement with medical concerns found in Manichaean asceticism totally belies its traditional interpretation in terms of spirit/matter duality or a disdain for all things bodily. In the Manichaean strain of asceticism, at least, the concerns of the body, and issues of its perfectibility and control, are actually exalted into a paradigm for the structure of the entire cosmos and the course of salvation history.

Rather than accept such a radical redefinition of Manichaeism, or face the collapse of our own discursive boundaries which it entails, it has been standard practice to marginalize discussion of Manichaean "science" and "ritual" and concentrate on mythological elements which are more amenable to manipulation as "metaphor." In the guise of translation, of putting the unknown in terms of the known, scholars engage in an ideological imperialism that re-cuts another culture's world to the shape of their own. The well-intentioned program of the history of religions has been to presume in others an intelligence like our own and to create a coherence for them on our own terms by applying the classification of metaphor to anything that does not fit our own sense of the real.[40] Unfortunately, this metaphorizing hermeneutic describes the Other "within the language and rhetorical system shaped by the conqueror" and is "intended to project (the conqueror's) presence and ascendency" (Burshatin: 212). In this way we not only violate the distinctive discursive

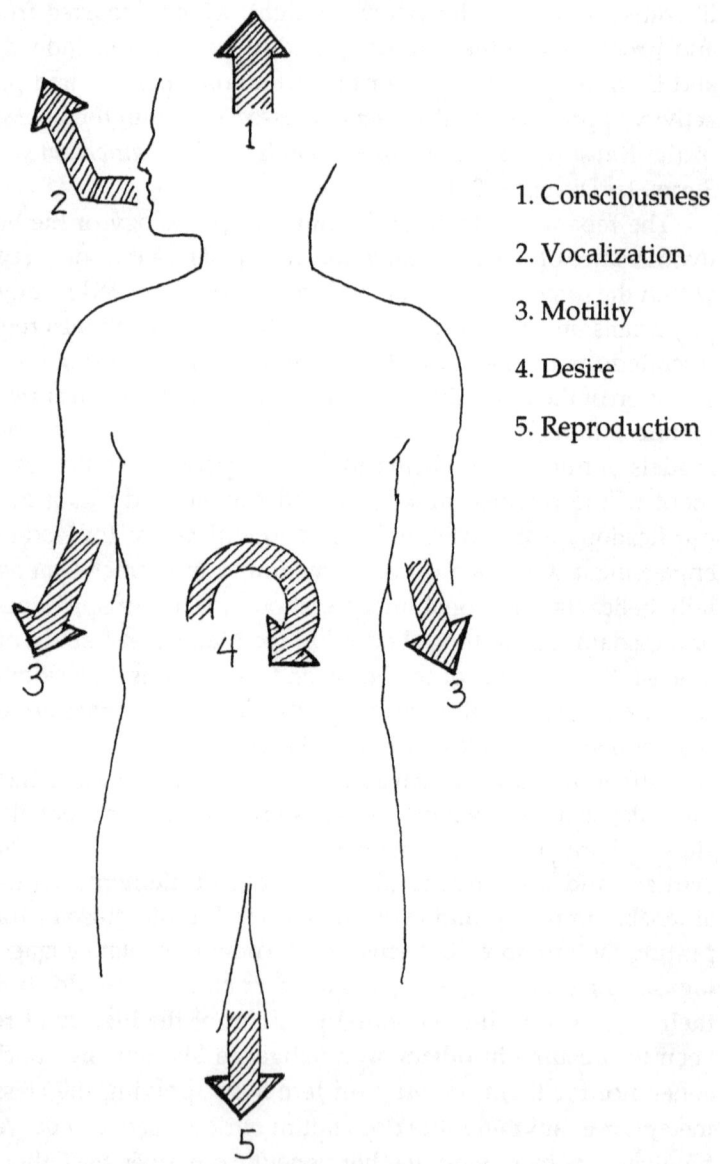

THE FIVE PRODUCTS OF FOOD (*Kephalaion* 104)

formations of another culture, but also rupture that culture's entire epistemic universe. We thus appropriate the language of the Other as a confirmation of our own paradigm and at the same time erase, marginalize, or misconstrue the Other's paradigm within which the language is actually employed.

Edwyn Bevan criticizes this tendency and explains that by such a metaphorizing hermeneutic,

> ... a claim is made to see behind the traditional belief a reality which can be better expressed or understood in other terms ... anyone who says that [utterances] are symbols may think he has a relatively clear view of the reality behind them, a reality differing from the symbol, if understood literally. And it is to these *beliefs* put forward as *substitutes* for the traditional affirmations that objection is raised (260, emphasis added).

For the interpretive assumption to be true, the *action* of the Other should reflect the presumed meaning (what the metaphor aims at) rather than the statement (the medium of the metaphor). When, however, the Other acts as if the statement is understood literally, the imperialistic interpretation is disproved, since "[n]o metaphor occurs where none is recognized ... there is no such thing as an unconscious metaphor" (Sandor: 103; for supporting arguments, see 111*f*.).[41] Hence the motivation to disparage or ignore ritual and practice by those engaged in interpreting (or appropriating) statements, and the divergent treatment of mythology over against ritual in the history of our field, which Jonathan Z. Smith has noted.[42]

A comparative example may be useful here, and Andras Sandor has supplied us with one. He cites the case of the Moche of Peru, whose artistic depictions of half-human, half-hummingbird figures, and of hummingbirds in association with athletes, could be characterized as a metaphorical relation. But in light of the fact that the Moche actually ate hummingbirds in order to acquire their special characteristics, we must conclude that this relation was not metaphorical to the Moche. Metaphorical relations cannot be metabolized, but actual relations (of this particular sort, anyway) can be. In the Moche example, as in the Manichaean case under discussion, it is an action which informs a representation, or visual statement, and defines it as direct, actual, "real," not metaphorical. We may very well "know" that no actual, direct relation can be physically established between the Moche and the hummingbird, or, in another of Sandor's examples, between the Kwakiutl and the salmon, but in their world these relations do exist, because their discourses about reality define the world in that way.[43] If we are to determine the character (locate the place and role) of statements within a discourse, or analyze and determine the distinctive relations among statements in a discourse, we must take the discourse on its own terms, within its own *episteme*.[44]

The Manichaeans would have been speaking metaphorically when they said that "salvation is digestion" if they had taught that *the point* of salvation is the separation of good from evil *as* digestion is the separation of nutriment from excrement. This would have been the construction of an intelligible analogical model by a tranference of statements from another discourse. But it is quite another thing to have said, as the Manichaeans did, that salvation is *the product* of digestion, that digestion is actually the separation of good from evil because both good and evil are *material substances mixed together in our food*, that pure digestion separates the good substance from the evil substance and sets it free, that digestion produces not just nutriment for the body but refines this still further into a conscious, divine exudation. This is no longer metaphor (or putting one thing in terms of another); it is identification—it is enunciated as a direct description of reality.

In his analysis of discursive formations, Foucault recognizes the distinction between these two modes of enunciation (1972: 57). Metaphors inhabit what Foucault calls the "field of concomitance," where statements "concern quite different domains of objects, and belong to quite different domains of objects, and belong to quite different types of discourse," but are employed within otherwise unrelated discourses "because they serve as analogical confirmation . . . or because they serve as models that can be transferred to other contents." Literal statements, on the other hand, occupy the "field of presence," which includes "all statements . . . taken up in a discourse, acknowledged to be truthful, involving exact description, well-founded reasoning, or necessary presupposition."[45] Manichaean statements about the body were central to the daily practices which established community identity and gave that community its *raison d'être*. These statements, therefore, belonged to the field of presence enunciated by Manichaean discourse. Physiological models from medical disciplines were taken up directly, and put in immediate relation to Manichaean ascetic and salvational themes.

Certainly, some parallels to this ascetic salvational language can be found in texts from other traditions which we regard as "religious" and these parallels have been, and in many cases perhaps should be, regarded as metaphorical. But we find stronger and more immediate parallels in medical and scientific texts, which belong in traditional estimation to discourses whose language is to be taken literally. The Manichaean statements we have been considering, like those of this latter group of "literal" discourses, are not bound to linguistic indicators of metaphor or analogy. In fact, the contemporaneous critics of Manichaeism frequently noted the absence of metaphoric or allegorical meaning in Manichaean statements. Simplicius reports:

> They mention some pillars, but they do not take them to mean 'that which holds heaven and earth together,' as they do not think it right to understand any of the things they say allegorically, but those [pillars] which are made of solid stone and carved, as one of their wise men informed me ... they fabricate certain marvels which are not worthy to be called myths. However, they do not use them as myths nor do they think that they have any other meaning but believe that all the things which they say are true [i.e. literal] (*In Epictetum Encheiridion* 27:71,44–72,15).[46]

The ancient polemicists, like us, were confronted with incongruent reality statements which they were prepared to treat "generously" and symbolically. They sought to bring Manichaean language into the parameters of their own discursive distinctions so that the Manichaeans could be comprehended in familiar terms, measured by these familiar terms, and refuted by their divergence or deficiency with respect to them.[47] Whereas we have abandoned the program of refutation as inappropriate in the history of religions, we still have not escaped the evaluation of another culture's language as part and parcel of our comprehension of it.[48] We are not prepared to deal with discordant realities, and this interpretive block has rendered the relations between ascetic discursive formations and ascetic practices problematic, not just in the case of Manichaeism, but possibly in the study of other ascetic traditions as well.

The Manichaean *episteme* arranges its discourses in patterns different from our own, and its apprehension of the world came into conflict both with traditions we consider religious and with those we term scientific (*Xuastvanift* IIC; Ephrem Syrus, *1st Discourse*, 22–23; Ferrari; Lieu: 449–454.). The Manichaeans knew full well what a metaphor was, and employed metaphors frequently in both poetry and prose (e.g., *Psalmbook*, *Hymn-Cycles*). But their cosmogony, cosmology, and soteriology also had concrete, literal statements which were not interpretively negotiable. "[S]ince Mani was the Last Prophet, and had brought the final revelation to humankind, there was no place left for interpretation or exegesis of his message. Hence Manichaeans were asked to believe his apodictic sayings and mythical doctrines *au pied de la lettre*" (Stroumsa and Stroumsa: 40).

> "The Manichaeans ... when they abandon their material fancies, cease to be Manichaeans ... the divine mysteries which were taught figuratively in books from ancient times were kept for Manichaeus, who was to come last, to solve and demonstrate; and so after him no other teacher will come from God, *for he has said nothing in figures and parables, but ... taught in plain, simple terms.* Therefore ... the Manichaeans ... have no interpretations to fall back on" (Augustine, *Contra Epistolam Fundamenti*, 23; emphasis mine).

These direct utterances grounded specific physical practices and, in fact, could only do so insofar as they were regarded as literal descriptions of reality.

By conceptually grounding their daily behavior in the fundamental structures of the universe, Manichaeans collapsed physics into metaphysics, physiology into cosmology, and dietetics into sacrality. At the same time, they apprehended the entire universe in all its many dimensions in the light of the regimen by which they lived. It was through this regimen, this code of relations, that the Manichaeans sought to control the universe in which they found themselves, and attempted to rectify the problematic givenness of their existence.[49] Ascetic discourse and ascetic practice developed by reciprocal relations, each structuring and informing the other, and together subsuming all other discourses and practices to a single comprehensive *episteme*. "Reality" is the end-product of this generative process, not the starting point. Though characterized as a world-renouncing occupation, asceticism itself constructs a world, a reality that can be controlled and comprehended—a physical solution to an existential crisis.

NOTES

[1] "Discursive practices are not purely and simply ways of producing discourse. They are embodied in technical processes, in institutions, in patterns for general behavior, in forms for transmission and diffusion, and in pedagogical forms which, at once, impose and maintain them" (Foucault, 1977b: 200). Throughout this paper, my analysis of Manichaean discourse utilizes categories and models drawn from Foucault (esp. 1972).

[2] According to Foucault, a discourse's "role among non-discursive practices" is not "extrinsic to its unity, its characterization, and the laws of its formation," but is one of its "formative elements" (1972: 67–68).

[3] E.g. the ascetic hyperbole of repugnance for the body in the Christian and Manichaean traditions, even though the former regards the body as the creation of God, and the latter holds that it is modeled on the perfect form of the deity.

[4] In this paper, I employ the literal/metaphorical distinction only in the strictest sense recognized by Lakoff. Literal here means "nonmetaphorical literality: directly meaningful language—not language that is understood, even partly, in terms of something else" (Lakoff:292). Metaphor can be defined as "a structural mapping from one domain of subject matter (the source domain) to another (the target domain)" (294). Understanding an utterance which employs metaphor requires a recognition of the transference from the source to the target domain, regardless of whether that transference is novel or conventional. When metaphors become conventional the source domain recedes from notice but the transferred character of the metaphor is no less recognized from its context of use. Not to recognize the contextual demand for metaphorization would result in dramatic misunderstanding. The conventionalization of metaphorical speech is a process of habituation over time and does not affect the requirements of metaphor production, namely, that "metaphoric predications cannot be *produced* and *noticed* unconsciously" (Sandor: 112, emphasis added).

5 "We speak of metaphor when we think or feel that an identification or predication in question cannot be literal, direct, because it is contrary to our experience and/or logic.... The very same verbal form (or visual presentation) may constitute a direct or a metaphorical predication according to one's beliefs" (Sandor: 101).

6 W. M. Urban explains that "the meaning we shall convey by the use of (a) word depends upon the acknowledgement of the presuppositions or suppositions which create these contexts or universes (of discourse).... In the case of meta-linguistic ambiguity the word can be understood only in a context which *goes beyond* the merely linguistic expression in which the word is found... it cannot be understood unless the individual hearing the word shares in the *presuppositions* which... *constitute* the context or universe of discourse in which the word has its meaning" (194–5). Cf. the work of Stanley Fish.

7 A quick survey in Liddell and Scott shows that the individual terms for which I have given the Greek are employed as technical vocabulary in Hellenistic medicine.

8 Except for particular statements of analogy or comparison, which will be marked by clear linguistic indicators, and the imbedded metaphors of conventional speech.

9 The sifting of language in a designated discourse into "metaphorical" and "literal" categories based on our own external expectations violates Urban's principle that "it is impossible to reduce context as universe of discourse to context of situation" (199). Scholars have only been able to metaphorize physical and physiological language in Manichaean and ascetic discourse, for example, by treating each utterance individually, or at most as a commonly employed trope, without acknowledging the set of relations which bind the individual utterances together into a universe of discourse.

10 "We universalize in the name of metaphor, forcing our own way of thinking, our logic, on others" (Sandor: 102).

11 According to Foucault, "it is usually the case that a discursive practice assembles a number of diverse disciplines or sciences or that it crosses a certain number among them and regroups many of their individual characteristics into a new and occasionally unexpected unity" (1977b: 200). The problem arises in determining what, in any given period, constitutes a discourse as opposed to a discipline or science, especially in periods and cultures removed from our own.

12 Compare the four bodily pollutants given here (blood, hunger, gases, flesh) with those of CMC 80–81 (blood, bile, gases, excrement). Cf. M9, M101, TM298. The Manichaeans are not known for consistency of ideological detail.

13 The purification of the bodies of the elect is the central axis of the entire elaborate cosmogony – anthropogony – soteriology schema of Manichaeism. See my comparison of the *Canjing* with *Kephalaion* 38 in "The Battle for the Body in Manichaean Asceticism" (forthcoming).

14 Edited and translated in C. H. Roberts, *Catalogue of the Greek and Latin Papyri in the John Rylands Library, Manchester*, Vol. 3 (Manchester, 1938): 38–46 (Text 469).

15 Augustine, *De Haeresibus*, 46, 114–16: "They believe that the souls of the Auditors are returned to the Elect, or by a happier short-cut to the food of their Elect so that, already purged, they would then not have to transmigrate into other bodies."

16 Compare the Hellenistic physician Asclepiades of Bithynia, who states that the "*solutio* of food appears in the belly and it passes through the various parts of the body, penetrating... all the fine passages.... It travels through the parts which accept nutriment, becoming now artery, now nerve, vein, or flesh" (Caelius Aurelianus, *De morbis acutis*, 1.113). The classification of body parts into a small number (anywhere from 4 to 7) of tissue-types was a commonplace, not only in the Mediterranean area, but also in Persia and India.

17 Henrichs and Koenen have suggested as a Biblical precedent which may have guided Mani's peculiar physiological conclusions Mark 7:18–19 (*ZPE* 32 [1978]: 137ff.). Nevertheless, Mani's language is medical, not Biblical. The term *oikonomia*, which I have left untranslated, essentially corresponds in medical discourse of this period to

our term "physiology," "the relation of (the body's) receipts to its expenditure" (Jones: 3).

[18] Keesing claims that "even if we were to find a ritual where, say, the living used fire or heated objects in order to induce the ancestors to do whatever it is they do, we could be seeing not the enactment of a folk theology of what ancestors do to effect changes in the world humans experience directly, but a *dramatization of the metaphorized homology between source and target domains*" (211, emphasis added). But Bevan points out that "any theory which tells you to act *as if* something were true, does, by very implication, assert the importance of truth of fact in regard to practice. . . . The rightness of conduct would depend directly on the truth of fact" (298).

[19] Cf. Galen, who quotes the *Timaeus*—"Attempt must be made as far as possible, by *trophē*, by occupations, and by education, to avoid evil, and choose its opposite"—and comments: "For since occupations and education are destructive of evil and productive of virtue, so also is *trophē*. And while *trophē* sometimes means not only food but the whole regimen . . . yet . . . in the present instance . . . by *trophē* one can understand nothing else than foods, broths, and beverages. . . . And if anyone wishes, independently of Plato, to know all about food values, he may read three books of my own on this subject, as also a fourth 'On Humours Good and Bad,'" (Brock, 1929: 242–3).

[20] The expressions "Hellenized" and "Platonized" (and one might well add "Gnosticized") are used conventionally, even though many Greek thinkers, including Plato, do not really adhere to typical spirit/matter dualism. "Platonized" here stands for Neo-Platonism, which arose contemporaneously with, and in distinct opposition to, Manichaeism.

[21] According to Edelstein, philosophers and physicians were "antagonists in the struggle for leadership in the conduct of life" (350). Cf. Simon: 267; Frede: 231–42; and Aristotle, *De sensu* 436a17–21; *De resp.* 480b28–30.

[22] Cf. Mani's defense before the shah Bahram, made entirely on the basis of his medical accomplishments, in M3.

[23] Apollonius of Tyana, as portrayed by Philostratus, is another example. See his *Life*, 1.8–9.

[24] Galen actually wrote a treatise against the Middle Platonists demonstrating the fact: "That the *dunameis* of the Soul follow the *crases* of the Body" (translated in Brock, 1929: 232–43).

[25] Cf. Plato, *Timaeus* : "Acid and saline phlegm and bitter bilious humours roam about the body, and if they are trapped inside and can get no outlet the vapour that rises from them mixes with the movement of the soul, and the resultant confusion causes a great variety of disorders . . ." (Lee: 117). Also Diogenes Laertius 8.23: "One should abstain from broad beans, since they are full of wind and take part in the soul, and if one abstains from them one's stomach will be less noisy and one's dreams will be less oppressive and calmer." Cf. *Breaths* 14.

[26] "Anonymus is preoccupied with the assimilation of food and with respiration. . . . Beginning with a brief anatomical account of the various parts of the body, the argument goes on to discuss *pneuma*, nutriment and the various emanations (*apophorai*) from the body. Special attention is paid to digestion, to the veins and arteries, and to the invisible 'pores'" (Jones: 3).

[27] A comparison of M101b with M9 II V shows that Manichaeans also thought the nerve/sinew (*pay*) to be filled with breath (*wād*). The same two texts show that veins (*rag*) carry blood (*xōn*). The parallel texts *Kephalaion* 38 (Coptic) and *Canjing* (Chinese) use the conventional terms for "sinew" and "nerve," respectively.

[28] Generations of scholars and physicians puzzled over the Hippocratic instruction that an enema is an alternative to venesection before it was understood that the excretory tract is part of the vascular system in ancient Mediterranean medicine (Saunders: 25).

[29] Cf. the Hippocratic *Sacred Disease*, 10; and the views of Diocles of Carystus in Phillips: 128.

30 According to Celsus, Asclepiades of Bithynia excluded medicines from his practice, and maintained and restored health primarily by dietetic means (Spencer, 2: 3). Cf. Frede: 228.

31 I.e., what Farb and Armelagos call a "cuisine." According to Ricoeur, "the division between the pure and the impure ignores any distinction between the physical and the ethical and follows a distribution of the sacred and the profane which has become irrational for us" (27).

32 One need only compare the Manichaean dietetic regimen with the remnants of Erasistratus' *Hygiene* (Wesley Smith). Both sought to reduce the pollution of the body by fasting and an easily digestible diet, which for Erasistratus included "garden vegetables . . . squash, cucumbers, ripe melons, green figs, some pulse . . . and unkneaded whole-wheat bread" (Smith:405)—a typical *Ruwanagan* menu. Cf. Hippocrates, *Aphorisms* 2.4: "The more you feed bodies that are not pure (*mē kathara*), the more you will harm them"; Stephanus of Athens: "in cases of bodies that are not clean (*akatharton*) no food should be administered until they have been purged (*katharseōs*), because otherwise from this food more matter (*hulē*) will be added to the bad humor" (Westerink: 155).

33 It could be argued that even this does not distinguish Manichaean from typical medical discourse. Vallance points out that the "characterization of disease as uniform, reducible to one type of explanation, has a long history, going back at least as far as those sophistic Hippocratic treatises such as *On Breaths*" (125). He adds that "sophistic showpieces like *On Breaths* did have their own intellectual progeny. Our picture of Hippocratism is so coloured by Galen that it is easy to forget the importance of this tradition" (146). This endeavor "to simplify the explanation of health and disease" is not confined to the Hippocratic tradition—which may itself rely upon Egyptian antecedents (Saunders and Steuer)—and is a part of every culture's quest for well-being.

34 "Whether a body is judged as healthy or sick is not a matter of observation. The 'facts' of health and unhealth become facts only in connection with some standards about how a body should perform . . . what comes to be regarded as knowledge about bodies is knowledge in the context of standards for those performances . . ." (Shapiro: 139).

35 We should not be misled by the use of *gnosis* in the CMC and elsewhere into thinking that this was a philosophized, abstracted, or merely mental (i.e., metaphorical) process of liberation. The special *gnosis* of the Manichaeans, as already noted for the passage under discussion by Buckley (1983), is the knowledge of the correct action, the knowledge of liberatory praxis. "The 'internalization' encountered in Manichaeism destroys immediate expectations of an equation between inner reality and purely theoretical *gnosis*. A metaphysical understanding of the separation between light and darkness does not suffice, the *real* differentiation goes on in the body" (335).

36 According to Galen, Nature itself has two powers (*dunameis*)—the attraction and assimilation of what is "appropriate" (*oikeion*) and the expulsion of what is "foreign" (*allotriōn*) (Brock, 1916: 45).

37 The contamination caused by meat-eating, for example, is said to sully the "soul," increase lust, and pollute the mouth, among other things (M177 R).

38 Semen as the final end-product of digestive filtration was a commonplace not only in Hellenistic medicine, but also in Persian and Indian belief.

39 A regimen, then, would fit Foucault's characterization of a "disciplinary technology" that produces a "docile body that may be subjugated, used, transformed, and improved" (Chidester: 3).

40 Ascription of metaphor is dependent upon two interpretive determinations: "not to accept literal meaning and not to accept absurdity or inanity" (Sandor: 108).

41 By metaphor in this context Sandor means active, not conventionalized, metaphorical utterance.

⁴² According to Smith, in the study of ritual "that which was 'other' remained obdurately so and, hence, was perceived to be bereft of all value. The 'other' displayed in ritual could not be appropriated as could myth and was therefore shown the reverse face of imperialism: subjection or, more likely, extirpation" (102). Ritual can also be extirpated more subtly, simply by being ignored.

⁴³ "A universe of discourse is ... conditioned by ... the assumption of the reality of the universe in which the discourse takes place. Mutual acknowledgment of that supposition is the condition of meaningful or intelligible discourse. The condition of the meaningfulness of an assertion or proposition is, then, *not* that certain entities about which the assertion is made exist, in the sense of being empirically verifiable, but that the universe of discourse in which these entities have their existence is mutually acknowledged" (Urban: 201).

⁴⁴ Episteme = "the total set of relations that unite, at a given period, the discursive practices that give rise to epistemological figures, sciences, and possible formalized systems" (Foucault, 1972: 191).

⁴⁵ Conventional metaphors are probably among the types of statements found in a third "field of memory," which contains inactive, obsolete language that has a parasitic or genetic relationship to the active language taken up into a discourse.

⁴⁶ Cf. Alexander of Lycopolis 10, p.16, 14–19: "Their stories are undoubtedly of the same sort [as those of the Greek myths] since they openly describe a war of *hulē* against God, and they do not even mean this allegorically, for example as Homer did, who, in his *Iliad*, describes Zeus' pleasure on account of the war of the gods against each other, thereby hinting at the fact that the universe is constructed out of unequal elements, which are fitted together and both victorious and vincible." Also, Augustine, *Contra Faustum* 16, 26. On this polemical response, see esp. Lieu.

⁴⁷ Often enough, the anti-Manichaean polemicists relented and engaged in debate on the Manichaeans' own (physical/physiological) terms. Note especially Ephrem Syrus, *1st Discourse*, 21–27; *2nd Discourse*, 31, 42ff.; Alexander of Lycopolis, 22. This was especially true in cases where the polemicist felt well-grounded in a superior science.

⁴⁸ But "predications should not be conceived as metaphoric whenever *it is acknowledged* that they were not intended and not understood as metaphoric. . . . If certain people need no metaphoric transfer to make sense of their own predications, we should not take refuge in such a transfer" (Sandor: 112). To deny the acknowledged intelligibility of an utterance within its discourse "would only be a denial from the perspective of another discourse" (Shibles: 56).

⁴⁹ It must be kept in mind that "salvation" embraces—not just for the Manichaeans but apparently for most people in this particular cultural milieu—not just "spiritual" issues and "ultimate concern" but also health, power, sexuality, sustenance: in short, issues of existential givenness which are perceived to require a resolution, a cure, a "fixing."

WORKS CONSULTED

Asmussen, Jes P.
    1965   *XUASTVANIFT: Studies in Manichaeism*. Copenhagen: Prostant apud Munksgaard.

Bevan, Edwyn
    1938   *Symbolism and Belief*. Gifford Lectures of 1933 and 1934 at the University of Edinburgh. New York: Macmillan.

Brock, Arthur John
    1916   *Galen: On the Natural Faculties.* Cambridge: Harvard University Press.
    1929   *Greek Medicine: Being Extracts Illustrative of Medical Writers from Hippocrates to Galen.* London: J. M. Dent and Sons.

Buckley, Jorunn Jacobsen
    1983   "Mani's Opposition to the Elchasaites: A Question of Ritual." Pp. 323–36, 713–15 in *Traditions in Contact and Change.* Ed. Peter Slater and Donald Wiebe. Waterloo: Wilfred Laurier University Press.
    1986   "Tools and Tasks: Elchasaite and Manichaean Purification Rituals." *JR* 66:399–411.

Burshatin, Israel
    1984   "Power, Discourse, and Metaphor in the Abencerraje." *MLN* 99:195–213.

Chavannes, Éduard and Paul Pelliot
    1911   "Un traité manichéen retrouvé en Chine." *JA* 18:499–617.

Chidester, David
    1986   "Michel Foucault and the Study of Religion." *RSR* 12:1–9.

Edelstein, Ludwig
    1967   *Ancient Medicine: Selected Papers of Ludwig Edelstein.* Ed. Owsei Temkin and C. Lilian Temkin. Baltimore: Johns Hopkins University Press.

Farb, Peter and George Armelagos
    1980   *Consuming Passions: The Anthropology of Eating.* Boston: Houghton Mifflin.

Ferrari, Leo C.
    1973   "Astronomy and Augustine's Break with the Manichees." *Revue des études Augustiniennes* 19:263–76.

Foucault, Michel
    1972   *The Archaeology of Knowledge.* Trans. A. M. Sheridan Smith. New York: Pantheon.
    1977a   *Discipline and Punish: The Birth of the Prison.* Trans. Alan Sheridan. New York: Pantheon.
    1977b   "History of Systems of Thought." Pp. 199–204 in *Language, Counter-Memory, Practice.* Ed. Donald F. Bouchard. Ithaca: Cornell University Press.

Frede, Michael
    1987   *Essays on Ancient Philosophy*. Minneapolis: University of Minnesota Press.

Gould, Josiah
    1970   *The Philosophy of Chrysippus*. Leiden: Brill.

Henning, Walter B.
    1936   "Ein manichäisches Bet- und Beichtbuch." *APAW*, 1936, no. 10.

Jones, W. H. S.
    1947   *The Medical Writings of Anonymus Londinensis*. Cambridge: Cambridge University Press.

Keesing, Roger M.
    1985   "Conventional Metaphors and Anthropological Metaphysics: The Problematic of Cultural Translation." *Journal of Anthropological Research* 41:201–17.

Lakoff, George
    1986   "The Meaning of Literal." *Metaphor and Symbolic Activity* 1:291–96.

Lee, Desmond, trans.
    1971   *Plato: Timaeus and Critias*. New York: Penguin.

Lieu, Samuel N. C.
    1985   "Some Themes in Later Roman Anti-Manichaean Polemics: I." *Bulletin of the John Rylands University Library* 68:434–72.

May, Margaret Talmadge
    1968   *Galen: On the Usefulness of the Parts of the Body*. Ithaca: Cornell University Press.

Mitchell, L. W.
    1912   *S. Ephraim's Prose Refutations of Mani, Marcion, and Bardaisan*. London: Williams and Norgate.

Phillips, E. D.
    1987   *Aspects of Greek Medicine*. Philadelphia: Charles.

Ricoeur, Paul
    1967   *The Symbolism of Evil*. Trans. Emerson Buchanan. New York: Harper and Row.

Sandor, Andras
　1986　"Metaphor and Belief." *Journal of Anthropological Research* 42:101–22.

Saunders, J. B. de C. M.
　1963　*The Transitions from Ancient Egyptian to Greek Medicine.* Lawrence: University of Kansas Press.

Shapiro, M. J.
　1981　*Language and Political Understanding: The Politics of Discursive Practices.* New Haven: Yale University Press.

Shibles, Warren
　1971　*An Analysis of Metaphor in the Light of W. M. Urban's Theories.* The Hague: Mouton.

Siegel, Rudolph E.
　1970　*Galen on Sense Perception.* Basel: Karger.
　1973　*Galen on Psychology, Psychopathology and Function and Diseases of the Nervous System.* Basel: Karger.

Simon, Bennett
　1978　*Mind and Madness in Ancient Greece.* Ithaca: Cornell University Press.

Smith, Jonathan Z.
　1987　*To Take Place: Toward Theory in Ritual.* Chicago: University of Chicago Press.

Smith, Wesley D.
　1982　"Erasistratus' Dietetic Medicine." *Bulletin of the History of Medicine* 56:391–409.

Spencer, W. G.
　1935　*Celsus: De Medicina.* Cambridge: Harvard University Press.

Steckerl, Fritz
　1958　*The Fragments of Praxagoras of Cos and his School.* Leiden: Brill.

Steuer, Robert O. and J. B. de C. M. Saunders
　1959　*Ancient Egyptian and Cnidian Medicine: The Relationship of their Aetiological Concepts of Disease.* Berkeley: University of California Press.

Stroumsa, Sarah and Gedaliahu Stroumsa
  1988   "Aspects of Anti-Manichaean Polemics in Late Antiquity and under Early Islam." *HTR* 81:37–58.

Telfer, William, ed.
  1955   *Cyril of Jerusalem and Nemesius of Emesa.* Library of Christian Classics 4. London: SCM.

Temkin, Owsei
  1977   *The Double Face of Janus and Other Essays in the History of Medicine.* Baltimore: Johns Hopkins University Press.

Urban, Wilbur Marshall
  1939   *Language and Reality: The Philosophy of Language and the Principles of Symbolism.* London: Allen and Unwin.

Vallance, J. T.
  1990   *The Lost Theory of Asclepiades of Bithynia.* Oxford: Oxford University Press.

Westerink, Leendert G.
  1985   *Stephanus of Athens: Commentary on Hippocrates' Aphorisms.* Corpus Medicorum Graecorum XI 1,3,1. Berlin: Akademie-Verlag.

OLD WATER IN NEW BOTTLES: THE CONTEMPORARY PROSPECTS FOR THE STUDY OF ASCETICISM

Geoffrey Galt Harpham
Department of English
Tulane University

I am very grateful to Vincent Wimbush for asking me to respond to papers, many of which I heard at the meeting of the American Academy of Religion/Society of Biblical Literature in November, 1990 in, of all places, New Orleans. Mr. Wimbush's invitation gave me the opportunity not only to meet others who are working the same side of the *laura* but also to say what I should have said in my book *The Ascetic Imperative in Culture and Criticism*. The moment I finished that book, I scourged myself for not having said something on Bentham, something on Schopenhauer, something on Baudelaire and Rimbaud, something on Flaubert and Mallarmé, some more on Wittgenstein, something on Adorno's *Negative Dialectics*, and on Adorno and Horkheimer's *Dialectics of Enlightenment*, lots more on the iconographical motif of the Temptations of St. Anthony, and on those of St. Michel, St. Paul, and St. Jacques—Foucault, de Man, and Derrida. The list of these omissions, and their accompanying penances, grows every time I think about that book, not least because of the accumulating evidence that the world is turning in the direction of asceticism (which, of course, renounces it).

I am thinking not only of the growing body of knowledge produced by historical specialists, some of whom were present in New Orleans, but also of somewhat more popularizing (a word used here in an entirely honorific sense) work by Peter Brown, Susan Ashbrook Harvey, Elaine Pagels, Robin Lane Fox, and others. At a still further remove from the literal desert, Elisabeth Wyschogrod's recent book *Saints and Postmodernism* (University of Chicago Press, 1990) indicates the evergreen currency of self-denial as a critical concept. This currency is good well beyond the boundaries of religious studies. Sanford Budick and Wolfgang Iser have recently edited *Languages of the Unsayable: The Play of Negativity in Literature and Literary Theory* (Columbia University Press, 1990), a text whose emphasis on ascetic silence echoes in a recent volume called *How to Avoid Speaking: Denials*, which contains lengthy and eloquent essays by, among others, Jacques Derrida and Frank Kermode, two promising recent converts to silence.

Indeed, silence, unsayability, negativity, loss, and so forth virtually dominate the scene of contemporary critical theory, which may account for why its detractors so often refer to it as a "desert." Other recent titles that might be listed in this inventory include *Under the Sign of Loss: Tradition in the Space of Negativity*; Andrej Warminski's *Readings in Interpretation*, which announces itself as an examination of the "non-truth of reading and writing," based on "a negative"; and Thomas Haskell's essay in a 1990 issue of *History and Society*, called "Objectivity is Not Neutrality: Rhetoric vs. Practice in Peter Novick's *That Noble Dream*," which begins with warm praise for asceticism as a scholarly virtue. "Morality is what suffers most from the devaluation of ascetic practices," Haskell argues, "but such practices are also indispensable to the pursuit of truth." To which we can only say, Amen.

In this vein, incidentally, I recall an article in the magazine section of the London *Sunday Times* in the first week of 1989 about an extraordinary woman, whose name I've involuntarily renounced, who, from her monastery in the North of England, had just completed a superb history of painting by women, and who doubtless would second Haskell's linkage of morality and truth through ascesis. And, parenthetically, I recently came across an article by the British philosopher Simon Critchley about Jean Genet's *The Thief's Journal*, where Genet is quoted as saying that *saintliness* is "le plus beau mot du langage humaine." A short while ago, I was delighted to see a book announced in a publisher's catalogue with the promisingly minimalist title, *Desert*. I had already filled out the order form when I noticed that it was listed in the "Moral Philosophy" section, which suggested that the book was misleadingly advertised, and actually concerned a concept both synonymically and homonymically allied with "dessert," and was therefore likely to be of no value whatsoever. My own colleague at Tulane, Alain Saint-Saens of the History Department, is working on the eminently valuable subject of "Nostalgia for the Desert" in sixteenth-century France. At the New Orleans meeting, I speculated that perhaps even Operation Desert Shield could be seen as a perverted form of such nostalgia; now in the wake of Operation Desert Storm I am disinclined to make the same joke. I would, however, urgently recommend that Saddam Hussein, George Bush, and other potential belligerents read Vaclav Havel's treatise on ascetic statecraft, *The Power of the Powerless*.

The religious subculture here in the swamps and bayous of Louisiana occasionally yields evidence of a powerful nostalgia if not for the desert, at least for the rhetorical style first developed in the desert as a way of explaining the persistence of the world, the flesh, and the devil. "In my mind I knew it was demon spirits. . . . It would grip my mind and I would fight it. I can't tell you the holding, the times, to that fence outside our house, weeping before God, saying 'Lord, You said You would not allow anything to be put on us any harder than we can bear.' . . . You can fight it, fight it in your brain, until those mental images push you, shove you and ultimately he will get you to do what he's trying to get you to do, because flesh is not equal to spirit." The author, to relieve the suspense, is not St. Jerome, as many might have guessed, but Jimmy Swaggart, explaining to his dwindling flock in Baton Rouge in October, 1991, about reports of his recent indiscretions in Indio, CA.

For me, however, the most compelling evidence for the contemporary renewal of ascesis is not documented in the bibliographies of academic enterprise; it is contained in an article by Molly O'Neill called "Party's Over: Self-Denial is Hot" (A-16) that appeared in my hometown paper, *The Times-Picayune*, on May 27, 1990. "'Non' is more than a prefix," O'Neill writes. "It has become a lifestyle."

> It is the dinner bell: non-fat ice cream, non-dairy spread, non-caffeine cola, non-alcoholic beer.
>
> It is the mating call: "Non-smoking, non-drinking prince seeks sober princess."
>
> The red circle with the slash has become the country's all-purpose problem-buster. . . .
>
> Self-denial is both a penance and a panacea [according to a Manhattan psychologist].
>
> "People are terribly ashamed of what they have done in the past and terribly afraid of the future."

O'Neil tracks restaurants that advertise what their food does not contain, political candidates who trumpet their non-support for issues, fortune cookies promising that "Your discipline will be rewarded," "no color mascara" and "non-ionic microspheres for the face," and other forms of negation. She concludes by mentioning a cartoon in *The New Yorker* that pictured a befuddled middle-aged man declining an invitation: "We'd love to," he says into his telephone, "but we had too much wine and cheese in the '80's."

The signs indicate, then, that ascesis is not an idea whose time has come, but one whose time has never gone. It is, in short, an excellent season for specialists and nonspecialists to engage in a dialogue that both have, until now, resisted. On the one side, nonspecialists in fields such as literary theory have been reluctant to investigate the historical antecedents of the practices and values they analyze and advocate; and on the other, historians have been averse to the kind of theoretical inquiries that might enable them to grasp more fully the implications of their material. What is needed, I believe, is a new humility on the part of the historical amateurs and a new boldness on the part of the historical professionals. What follows, then, are the rather ad hoc reflections of an amateur, humbly addressed to professionals whose "boldness of speech," as Leif Vaage calls it, I would encourage.

One of the defining marks of the professional historian is an ascetic reluctance to speculate beyond the point warranted by documentary evidence. Without questioning the value of this reluctance, I would like to suggest that a number of these essays might profit from an infusion of small doses of "eremitic" extravagance. Carol Newsom's paper is an instance where a pivotal insight might be profitably pushed just a bit further in order for it to achieve its true dimensions, its full realization. The opening invocation of Foucault—who asks, "How have certain kinds of interdictions required the price of certain kinds of knowledge about oneself? What must one know about oneself in order to be willing to renounce anything?"—certainly suggests a spacious inquiry. But the application of this question to the Qumran community and its "session of the many," while fascinating on its own terms, is strictly and specifically historical, rather than, say, speculative.

But there are, I think, signs even within Newsom's text that the material strains towards generalization. According to Newsom, the practices at Qumran enforced or perhaps even produced a "curious bifurcation" of subjectivity, a dividedness thematized as warfare. Especially in contrast to the unity of voice with experience putatively exemplified in the Psalms, this bifurcation seems in every respect curious, aberrant, even perverse, or, as she says, "masochistic." But, scanning the history of the world, I wonder if the opposite case could be made, that it is psychic unity and wholeness rather than division that are exceptional. As a goal, aspiration, or wish, certainly unity has powerful claims; but the failure to achieve unity has far more powerful claims to being normative, and it is the distinction of the ascetic precisely to aspire *endlessly*. The condition engendered by this programmed frustration might be called "masochism," or it might be called "life."

To marginalize ascesis as masochism is to presume the normativity of unity. But this normativity is brought into question in the comment of Max Weber on which Foucault was trying, in his formulation, to improve. Weber was asking about what part of oneself one should renounce as the ascetic price of reason. Perhaps the most interesting implication of this question is the bland presumption that the self *has* parts, that these parts are discontinuous and can be pitted against each other, and that a genuine value—and even, perhaps, a kind of pleasure—attaches to the negation of one part by another. If ascesis, in its irrationality, produces reason, and if it feels good as well as bad, then—believe it or not—the case for a normative unity of experience would have neither truth nor desire to recommend it.

In saying this, I am encouraging Newsom not to be reluctant to proclaim the Qumran communicants proto-postmodernists. Nor the postmodernists as neo-ascetics. For the latter case, the evidence is plentiful. Michel de Certeau once reported that Jacques Derrida spent three months a year in a Cistercian monastery. This factoid has a species of confirmation in Derrida's work—its scrupulosity, its elaborate deference towards the text, its corresponding effacement of various notions of human subjectivity or bodiliness, its extreme skepticism with respect to certitude or plenitude. Derrida's colleague Paul de Man is ascetic through and through: everything de Man ever wrote bespeaks not only the recognizable ascetic values, but especially the kind of bifurcation, wrought in infernally complex figures, that Newsom notices at Qumran. De Man especially prizes the sacrifice of the unitary self as the condition of validity of knowledge, so much so that, among the tributes and attacks that poured forth after his death, the one to which most people refer, the one that seemed perhaps most persuasive as a summation of de Man's accomplishment, was named, simply, "Renunciation" (By Minae Mizumura, in *Yale French Studies*, 1984)

In fact, postmodernism could be said to begin with Foucault's interest in the *positive* effects of power-saturated discourses, as exemplified in contained communities, where "normalizing examination," "hierarchizing observation," definitions of "perversion," and so forth, were most conspicuously effective. As a point of fact, it is when Foucault realizes, while writing the first volume of the *History of Sexuality*, that insititutions are not invariably penal in character, that they do not all repress, that even carceral institutions do not simply produce suffering—it is at that moment (but really, the contributors to this volume might argue, a couple of millennia earlier) that postmodernism is born. For as the practices of Qumran, for example, in their very "curiosity," demonstrate, the effects of regulation on the subject can accord with desire—in this case, the desire for order, system, and code.

It cannot be simply a coincidence that Foucault reconceived his projected History of Sexuality series, taking it back rather than forward in time, as was his original plan, while at Berkeley, where one of his closest colleagues was Peter Brown. I'd like to ask Brown about this, and would urge Brown and others at Berkeley to write about it, for my suspicion is that in the climate of Brown (and of California), Foucault began to see the urgency of what has mistakenly been called a "return to Greece." The mistake lies in the overvaluation of Greece, when it was clearly the Christian communities of the third, fourth, and fifth centuries that provided the crucial inspiration. True, the volume eventually published as volume 2 of the series concerns Greece, but the second volume in order of composition—the one that reflects most clearly the turn or "return" of the new plan—remains unpublished. Foucault refers to it in late interviews, where he speaks at length about the importance to his thinking of Christian spirituality and ascetic practices in the time of Tertullian, Augustine, St. Anthony, and—Qumran.

It is certainly worth pointing out how many of the papers in this collection owe either an implicit or an explicit debt to Foucault. Kelsey, BeDuhn, Valantasis, and Corrington, as well as Newsom, are all working with methods, concepts, or categories that have devleoped in the wake of Foucault. This is nothing to be surprised at, and certainly not to be critical of, for Foucault was, among other things, the leading exponent of ascetic values and concepts among the major intellectuals of our time. To work in a "Foucauldian" vein is, therefore, entirely appropriate for those interested in understanding historical asceticism.

In general, therefore, I would urge those interested in asceticism to pursue investigations into such subjects as the decentered self as a specifically ascetic figure, one that emerged into high visibility in early Christianity, but which recurs throughout history in the less heavily coded forms of self-awareness, self-criticism, self-regulation, self-transcendence, and self-knowledge. (One figure for decenteredness might even be the riotous and scandalous marginal illustrations in medieval Psalters, which complicate the Psalms.) "Genuine masochism" might be seen to be more widespread than had previously been suspected; but additionally, the various rigors of institutional asceticism may come to seem more representative, more general in their implications than has been supposed. I would like to see Newsom and others expand the parameters of ascesis, to remove from it the stigma of being "curious." I, for one, from a comfortable seat on the fifty-yard line, will be cheering them on.

Ultimately, however, I am suggesting not just an enlargement of Newsom's argument, but a specific elaboration of it. Surely, the element of self-abuse, even self-torture, constitutes an element of "otherness" in early Christian asceticism. But to see the decenteredness which it radicalizes and amplifies as a far more widespread, maybe even universal and essentially ahistorical, phenomenon, is to see discourses such as those of Qumran as particularly glaring instances of a condition that, without such a caricature, might escape notice, or appear unexceptional. It is, I would argue, the historical importance and enduring power of ascetic discourse to underscore precisely those social and epistemic circumstances that prevail outside the walls of the monastery that makes that discourse so urgent and revealing, so worthy of the task of historical investigation.

Asceticism, we must remind ourselves, structures the very practices with which we attempt to understand it—pre-eminently, in historiography. It is in James E. Goehring's "Through a Glass Darkly: Diverse Images of the *APOTAKTIKOI(AI)* of Early Egyptian Monasticism" that I found the premises of historiography most clearly in evidence. With respect to the specific content of Mr. Goehring's paper, I have little to contribute other than my gratitude. For in my own pseudo-researches, I had confined myself almost entirely to "literature," or what he calls "theological propaganda," and so had ignored an entire dimension of ascetic practices. And his caution against taking a single source, or kind of source, as the only source is, I believe, a laudable and necessary reminder of one of the ascetic premises of scholarship itself, which entails a continual and principled submission of the subject to the evidence. Mere interpretations must remain vulnerable to being overturned by counterexamples and by the weight of evidence; and as one can never accumulate all the evidence, one must, as a scholar, remain prepared to abandon whatever thesis one has arrived at, no matter how cherished or hard-won.

Believing this, as I do, on the basis of ascetic convictions, I am less persuaded by Mr. Goehring's claim that documents can ever, as he says, "tell their own story." A comparison of sources can produce a healthy skepticism concerning the adequacy of any of them, but can such skepticism ever yield an absolutely adequate reconstruction of the event in itself, the pretextualized, preinterpreted thing, the object, as he says, "uncolored by preconceived notions"? I believe, rather, that the ascetic basis of scholarship would compel a structural skepticism as an analogue of the temptation that dominates man's life on earth. In fact, Mr. Goehring seems to believe this, too, to judge from his last paragraph.

But setting that aside, I am much more interested by the differences Goehring describes between "literary" documents and "documentary documents," differences that clarify in an especially productive way the nature of "literature." Where literature gives us eremites and cenobites, Goehring says, documentary documents tell of the less spectacular figure of the urban monk, quietly denying himself in his own village. Reading of this nearly-invisible form of asceticism, I began to suspect that one of my most cherished arguments, that ascesis represents a caricature of ordinary practices, and of fundamental social and psychic structures, was imprecise. In light of Mr. Goehring's arguments, it seems, rather, that the function of caricature must be attributed to the forms of ascesis documented in literature rather than to ascesis as such.

But perhaps my argument can be saved if I could harmonize myself with Mr. Goehring, and say that the ahistorical function of "literature" seems exactly analogous to the conceptual use I would like to make of historical asceticism. Both foreground through exaggeration a "break" that might otherwise have escaped notice or real understanding because of its nonabsolute, though still decisive, character, its ability to coexist with the ordinary life of the community, what Goehring calls its relatively "blurred" or "fluid" nature. We are now in the vicinity of a more profound argument than either of us has made, that literature and ascesis are coordinate forms, especially in the fundamental dimension of *emphasis*; and that this common function of emphasis, rather than just a mutual investment on the part of asceticism and narrative in temptation (as I had argued), accounts for the extraordinary historical influence of hagiography in the evolution of narrative.

Near the end of his paper, Mr. Goehring asks whether the experience of monastic or solitary life "call[ed] forth literary production as a means of self-evaluation. Contrariwise," he asks, "does the activity of an ascetic within a village work somehow against his or her literary productivity?" I believe that this provocative question has an answer. The history of literature is written by people who have made a kind of renunciation of the world, who have invested themselves in an alternate space within the world in order to clarify, explore, or understand themselves and their circumstances. World-hating Biblical prophets in both testaments merely exemplify a general condition of authorship, a kind of critical detachment that enables them, as Sir Philip Sidney—to take an instance as far removed from, say, Isaiah as possible—comments in his "Apology for Poetry," to "grow a second nature." This capacity to create a second world, which is taken as definitive of literature even today by, for example, V. S. Pritchett and many others, still seems to require a withdrawal from "the world" as its precondition. Maybe the urban monks produced no literature because their physical and psychic withdrawal from the first nature was not radical enough to encourage or permit them to create a second.

The literal necessity of making an ascetic break in order to create "literature" enables me to glimpse a further implication of my own argument with respect to narrative as "the ascetic form of discourse." As I noted a moment ago, I had argued in my book that narrative, both structurally and thematically, pivoted on the experience of trial or temptation. The condition of narrative temptation now appears to me structured by the *ambivalence* of the ascetic break from a world with which, as Goehring, Wimbush, BeDuhn and others in this collection point out, ascesis itself is not altogether incompatible. It is, in other words, the possibility that the ascetic-*cum*-creative break is not and need not—and perhaps even can not—be total or utter that places the creation structurally in the circumstance of trial, of simultaneous attraction and rejection, indebtedness and autonomy.

Historical asceticism can, then, be considered an early recognition and management of a certain "literary" dimension of life, a dimension both embedded within the ordinary as a difference, and taking the character of a schism, albeit one that is already at work within ordinariness. What "literature" confirms is the *exemplary* character of ascetic practices, the fact that ascesis can and ought to be imitated. Imitating ascesis in literature, Athanasius' *Life of Anthony*, for example, redoubles the "iterability" that is already visible in the actual material life of Anthony, and even traceable in the gray rupture of urban ascesis, and even written in invisible ink, as it were, in our very nature as created beings.

What I'm leading up to is the statement that literature does not *just* represent, as Goehring argues, the "inner world" of the monks' "self-understanding," although it does that brilliantly. It also makes ascesis identifiable and comprehensible as the deepest source of narrative, and perhaps of creation, itself. In doing so, literature takes ascesis out of the world of the inner self-understanding of a few and into the larger world from which the monks had departed, but which they cannot help illuminating. Indeed as Kelsey's marvelous discussion of the "body as desert" in *The Life of Anthony* suggests, the metaphorical (and therefore "literary") sharing of attributes between the individual and the larger world was a primary trope of asceticism from the beginning.

The lesson for the historian might be that neither the nonliterary nor the literary documents tell their own stories, for both must be taken as collaborators in the construction of a common story. The nonliterary accounts describe a fluid and relatively homogeneous social scene which contains without crisis a group of people who, though still within the village, had gently departed from it. The literary accounts paint a more lurid picture, stressing the ideology that underwrote that departure. Together, they image a way of life that works both within and against society; and it is this image that, I believe, most adequately expresses the essence of asceticism.

Verna Harrison's paper raises, in an especially direct way, the linked questions of ascetic practice, exegesis, sexuality, and figurality. Just as—Harrison implies—the ascetic sought to be "filled with the presence of Christ," so does the exegete seek to be "filled" with the allegorical or hidden meaning. This ideology of the human person as receptacle, incomplete in itself and awaiting fulfillment by another, actually destabilizes the patriarchy that asceticism supposedly articulates and propogates by making the female the representative of the species in its highest moments of aspiration. The relatively quiet moment in Harrison's paper where she states this recalls, for me, Mary Daly's subversive appropriation in *Gyn-Ecology* of the terms of the patriarchy; her term "hag-iography," for example, both borrows and overturns the patriarchal element of asceticism—without, I hasten to point out, overturning asceticism itself.

Harrison points provocatively to the persistence within Gregory of Nyssa's rhetoric of images of food and sex, images that, as Harrison says, must be interpreted allegorically because they are "pastorally inapplicable in their literal sense." According to Harrison, such images were employed because they activated strong and natural desires that could then be transcended or turned towards heavenly rather than earthly ends—"redirected and fulfilled, not extinguished." I wonder, however, if this interpretation, which is powerful in its orthodoxy and altogether orthodox in its power, is the only one.

Without contesting Harrison's thesis, I would like to contribute another, which I see not as a competitor but rather as—to retrieve an image from the discussion of Mr. Goehring's paper—a collaborator. Indeed, collaboration is the issue in a discourse that propagandizes for the immaterial and spiritual through a rhetoric of carnality and gratification. For what figurality, in its ambivalent suspension of the literal, enables the reader to do is in effect to have his cake and renounce it too. Figurality permits a kind of gratification of desire even as it figures, almost literally, a renunciation of desire. Figurality might, in other words, be the agent within an ideology of progress of an equal and opposite force of reaction, one that prizes allegory for the wrong reason.

Harrison would like to preserve the rightness of the right reasons, but what she almost says is that asceticism manages desire by mobilizing one part of desire against another part in a struggle whose outcome is not only not guaranteed, but not even truly sought. The desire invoked by ascetic discourse is, as Newsom states, structurally and permanently divided. Instead of Harrison's phrase "ascetical and iconic," I would propose, therefore, "ascetical and ironic." I am not, once again, trying to repudiate, much less mock, the otherworldly claims of the community of believers. I am simply trying to account for the powerful element of desire in the discourse, and in the worldly project, of asceticism. The very fact that, as Harrison says, it is "impossible to prevent inappropriate thoughts from entering the mind" compels one to try to provide some such account. Pastorally inapplicable though they were in their literal sense, images of food and sex may yet have provided a merciful refuge for desires so powerful that they simply could not be rejected in any utter or uncompromising form. If "the same human drive that impels one toward bodily love can also be directed toward God," then the reverse would surely also be true, and one could love God with "the same" love as one would direct towards one's significant embodied other. Figurality makes it possible, in a certain sense, to be an ascetic with*out* renunciation. I would, in a word, credit the powerful case made by Jason David BeDuhn concerning the transgressive literality of ascetic speech as an equally powerful component of the "regimen of salvation."

Ascetic discourse described in this way, which I imagine Harrison would reject, would serve as a kind of template over a host of other discourses whose project is the management rather than the denial of carnal desire. Psychoanalysis would be one of these, a practice in which the lurid rehearsal of one's story gratifies the desires embedded in it even as it supposedly liberates the subject from desire itself. Hermeneutics would be another, taking the form of a constantly renewed effort to stipulate the means and ends by and towards which a readerly desire is harnessed. In my own work, I argued that all interpretation theory can be seen as founded upon some version of the confrontation between a reactionary readerly desire and the stern imperative of the text, or the community, or the author's intention, or some other representative of the check on desire that is manifest in Gregory's, as in Augustine's, discourse by God's truth.

This brings us to allegory itself, which Paul de Man, the most thoroughly ascetic of all modern exegetes, advanced as the most bracing of literature's disciplines precisely because, in it, the reader was not "fulfilled," because meaning was always elsewhere. De Man opposed allegory to symbol, in which the aesthetic unity of sensuous form and inner meaning was achieved. For de Man, allegory was ethical because it rebuked the reader's desire for unity and fulfillment—although, as one might expect with de Man, it's a lot more complicated than that. But with the help of Harrison's paper, I can see now more clearly the ideology of the human-subject-as-receptacle that silently informed de Man's view of allegory, and can even see a canceled ideology of gender that informs allegory itself—an ideology that would have been a great scandal to de Man, who hardly needed another.

Writing "from the margins of established scholarship," Vincent Wimbush again raises questions about the quality of "literary sources" concerning early Christian asceticism. Wimbush argues that the ascetic community used accounts of "Ethiopian Moses" for propaganda purposes, and drew upon prevailing racial stereotypes in doing so. I would very much like to know more about these stereotypes and assumptions, and what other evidence there is for them, and Wimbush certainly has a rich and promising field opening out before him.

Perhaps the most interesting aspect of Mr. Wimbush's discussion to a non-historian is the emphasis he places, along with others in this collection, on the worldliness of putatively "unworldly" practices. For Wimbush, the "loss of world" ethos was charged with political energies that were dramatically highlighted in the case of Ethiopian Moses, whose race was considered an obstacle to true piety, and whose conversion therefore represented an especially telling instance of the power of ascetic practices and of the grace of God. "This ascetic orientation to the world," Wimbush writes, "was understood to parallel the foreignness that dark-skinned peoples" were considered to have "by those transmitting the tradition to experience." So Ethiopian Moses is in a sense both a radical instance of the power of faith coupled with practice, and an altogether exemplary case of a man renouncing the body in favor of the soul.

Despite Wimbush's insistence that asceticism is an ideology of absolutes, the material he is dealing with is so rich and complex that I wonder if any internally consistent account of it would be capable of rendering all its implications. Reading his essay, I am put in mind once again of Newsom's account of ascetic decentering and internal division. It is even possible to regard the story of Ethiopian Moses as an amplification of the already highly amplified antinomies of an ascetic ideology of self-division. Treated in this way, the story would still have propoganda value, but the case for which it would serve as propaganda would be slightly different. By showing how the power of God was capable of converting *even* a black man, Palladius and his successors could prove the magnificence of God on a particularly hard case. Thus race would be played off against grace; the story would both confirm popular racial prejudices *and* subvert them by showing how race could simply be negated by the power of faith and ascetic practices. The effectiveness of these would be proven by the way in which they controverted the plain evidence of the senses, especially against this particular "body" of evidence. Asceticism would, in this secondary or shadow-reading, present a point of view from which the category of race was instrumental only insofar as it could be shown to be negligible.

Karen Jo Torjesen tells a story somewhat comparable to Wimbush's, one in which the "discourse of praise" accorded to ascetic heroes enforced not an ideology of race but rather an ideology of virility. According to Torjesen, when ascetic women were described as exemplary, the examples were structured on a model of distinctively male virtue. This fact would be unsurprising to many, who regard asceticism as the historical speciality of the transcendental male. As a nonspecialist, however, I note without judgment that Gail Paterson Corrington outlines a considerably more expansive and specific role in asceticism for women, who took upon themselves the task of creating a defined and impenetrable body, leaving to men the project of keeping the body—and its fluids—within its established boundaries. If we accepted both Torjesen and Corrington's cases, then we could argue that while asceticism generated local effects of exclusion and privileging, the total effect of asceticism was not just to exclude, but rather to articulate a general and complex system within which various exclusions and privileges could occur, not all of which would be consistent with each other. In highly qualified priase of asceticism, we could say that while Torjesen's case that a woman could achieve honor only by in effect "becoming a man" is undeniably true, it is also the case that asceticism, through its cenobitic branch, developed a special category of virtue that appears to be modeled on the feminine virtues, as some have defined them, of community, non-competitiveness, and sharing. Thus, when Torjesen notes that "Women's praise is generic, for virtues they all share, while men are praised for their individual exploits," this does not necessarily imply that asceticism devalues women; it could well mean that women occupy a special place within an ascetic discourse of praise whose parameters are more spacious than Torjesen seems to believe. It is, incidentally, interesting to note the subsequent development in medieval Christianity of a special discourse of praise of Mary, patroness of ascetics, as "unique among all women," even while it was femininizing men as more or less interchangeable "Brides of Christ."

Wimbush provides another example of the spaciousness of asceticism, even while he notes its undeniable exclusionary effect. On one occasion the archbishop tells Moses, "Behold, you have become completely white, Father Moses"; to which Moses replies, "Indeed, the outside, O Lord Father; would that the inside were also white." Wimbush characterizes this exchange as "officially sanctioned hassling of Moses on account of his racial and color difference." Without really quarreling with this view, I would propose as an addition another interpretation, one that draws on both Harrison's argument for the metaphoricity of ascetic discourse and BeDuhn's argument for its literality. The archbishop's comments indicate that while color is indeed an issue, it is susceptible to metaphorization, so that literal black could, by virtue of piety, be figural white. Moses may have scorned his own skin because it is black, and this may indicate a general scorn for blackness in the literal and figurative senses; but Moses' self-contempt is also exemplary for those who would scorn their own skins, which are, in the eyes of God, also "black." The lesson would be, oddly enough, that it is not enough to appear to be "white" on the outside; one must also strive to make the inside equally "white." Precisely by virtue of his Blackness, Moses is exceptionally well positioned to teach others how to transform blackness into whiteness by treating their own external or bodily form with the contempt that even non-ascetic whites reserved for blacks.

Wimbush himself is well positioned here to undertake a critique of essentialism from an ascetic point of view. For while essentialisms are all reductive and potentially unjust, the ascetic essentialism sets race and—*pace* Harrison, Torjesen, and Corrington—gender essentialisms against themselves, deploying them in the destabilization of the prejudices they seem to reflect. This would produce the, for me, satisfying result that asceticism itself would be seen as not having a particular political valence, a predictable political effect: it could be at once a reactionary and a dynamically progressive force. Which one it turned out to be would depend upon the local configurations of force in a given circumstance. Wimbush might collaborate with BeDuhn, Harrison, Valantasis, and Kelsey on a study of "the making of the ascetic body," a project that would include a study of the ways in which the ascetic, the desert, and the demons swapped literal and metaphorical attributes in a process of reciprocal and mutual world-construction.

The original meaning of "renunciation," as Mr. Goehring reminds us, is to take leave of, to part with. Renunciation is thus a figure for a condition of being *in medias res*, distanced from an origin; or, by a slight extension, of being different from the objects of one's desire or knowledge; or even of aspiring towards a justice that remains elusive. And so forth, on out to all the forms and conditions of division and resistance that characterize and condition human existence, and that, really, provide whatever unity "human existence" has. Renunciation is made explicit in asceticism, and developed into a program of principled rigor, into an ethic in which those fundamental, indeed primordial, circumstances are transposed into the key of consciousness and even ideology.

This is the source of the historical and conceptual value of asceticism: it dramatizes in a flamboyantly marginal and yet critical way certain central features of the human condition. However it is defined, the problem of asceticism is, as Prof. Vaage says, "eminently our problem." The challenge facing students of asceticism is to dare to expand their conceptual field beyond the terms of the texts and the historical self-understanding possible to early Christians, to consider as crucial to an understanding of their subject such fields as ethics, psychoanalysis, language, political theory, gender formation, and racial categories, and to make the case that in the historical particularity of ascetic practices and institutions lies the germ and essence of much else. The task for specialists, a task well begun here, is to apply their expertise to those extended practices of ascesis remote from the desert but intimate to all of us.

Glossary

Anapausis—the Greek word meaning "rest." In Manichaeism it was used to refer to the radical discipline of non-interaction, or "rest" from mental duplicity, oral defilement (both dietetic and oral), violence (broadly defined), desire, and economic and socio-political concerns demanded of the elect. Since according to many forms of ascetic piety humans become entangled in the world through their harmful action in it, the only solution is a complete stoppage of such action.

Anachōrēsis—the Greek word for "withdrawal." The monk withdraws from the normal social, religious, political and familial relationships in order to live in solitude and focus attention on contemplation and prayer as both strategy and end.

Anachōrētēs—the Greek word meaning "one who withdraws." In English the term usually used is anchorite.

Anorexia Nervosa—a Greek medical term describing a severe loss of appetite that has no apparent physical cause, but long associated with the abstinences of ascetics.

Apotaktikos—a Greek term meaning "one who renounces." It is used as a label for certain ascetic Christians in the fourth century.

Binah/Binatka—the Hebrew for "understanding"/"understanding (that comes from) you." An important theme in Qumran literature.

Boundedness—an image schema that proceeds from the basic corporeal experience of physical containment (e.g. inside/outside). On the one hand, the body can be experienced as a container within which certain things can be placed (e.g. food and water), on the other hand, out of which certain other things flow (e.g. urine, sweat, blood, saliva). At the same time, the body can be experienced as an object that can move in and out of various containers (e.g. rooms, vehicles, clothes).

Coenobitism—from the Greek terms *koinonia*, "community," *koinos*, "common," a form of ascetic practice characterized by communal lifestyle and subordination of the individual will to a shared "rule" or pattern of life. In Christian tradition the Pachomian coenobium is perhaps prototypical. (See *koinonia* below.)

Conciliar Acts—records of the proceedings of ancient Christian councils, published either as stenographic transcriptions or, more commonly, as a series of formal resolutions or "canons" whose literary form is modeled on that of the published opinions of the Roman Senate.

Deliberative Rhetoric—one of the three major types of rhetorical speech known in classical antiquity, used typically within political debates in a council or assembly. Other types of rhetorical speeches were judicial (as might be used in a court of law) and epideictic (as might be used on public commemorative occasions).

Disappearance (of the body)—the normal relationship of a healthy person's consciousness to his/her body. In the normal everyday mode of experience the body is simply absent, not perceived. This disappearance applies to the exterior body components (e.g. arms, legs, head) and interior components, or visceral organs (e.g. stomach, lungs, heart, brain). The disappearance of the exterior body is referred to as "background disappearance," while the disappearance of the visceral components of the body is referred to as "depth disappearance."

Dys–appearance (of the body)—a state in which the body is perceived as problematic because of the presence of disease, suffering, pain, old age, and death. The prefix "dys" means "bad," "hard," or "ill" in Greek. Thus, the phenomenon of *dys*appearance means that the normally *absent* body now *appears*, but in a grossly abnormal condition.

Encratite—from the Greek term *enkratēs*, "self-controlled," the term is used as a label for certain Christians of antiquity who practiced rather strict or rigorous forms of asceticism.

Enthusiasmos—Literally "having the deity within," a Greek term that describes a state of spiritual possession.

Eremetism—from the Greek term *eremia*, "solitude," a form of ascetic practice characterized by communal lifestyle and the cultivation of individual perfection. Anthony is, perhaps, the prototypical eremite in Christian tradition.

Hagneia—a Greek term referring to ritual purity, usually requiring abstinence from sexual relations for a period of time in order to approach, or to be approached by, a deity.

Halakah—in Judaism, rules of conduct based on religious law or custom, and considered to be a restatement of the Torah (the first five books of the Hebrew Bible).

Hesychia—the Greek word meaning "quiet," or "rest." It denotes the state of ascetic stability and quiet. The quiet emerges from withdrawal from society, the stilling of the passions and focus upon ideals or goals (whether God or happiness, as among Greek philosophers and moralists).

Hodayah—a type of psalm or prayer of thanksgiving developed in the Qumram community. The term is derived from the introductory formula with which many of the compositions begin: "I thank you, O Lord," or "I thank you, my God."

Image Schemata—basic orientational metaphors that are structured and maintained by corporeal experiences. They make up that component of perception that lies within the perceiver and subsequently determines how objects and events in the physical world are perceived. They are not fixed, but are constantly modified by new information from personal experiences.

Inclusio—a literary device in which similar words or phrases appear at the beginning and end of a section of a text.

Koinōnia—from the Greek word *koinos*, "common," it is a reference to community. Often used as a technical term in the sources of Pachomian monasticism to refer to its particular system of affiliated monasteries. (See *Coenobitism* above.)

Maskil—an office in the Qumran community. It is associated primarily with the instruction of novices and members with liturgical functions.

Masochism/Masochistic Subjectivity—the term "masochism" is used here in the way Peter Berger suggests in *The Sacred Canopy*: ". . . the attitude in which the individual reduces himself to an inert and thinglike object *vis-à-vis* his fellowmen, singly or in collectivities or in the nomoi established by them. . . . Its key characteristic is the intoxication of surrender to another—complete, self-denying, even self-destroying" (55).

Metabolic Salvation—according to Manichaeism, a materialistic solution to the conflicts inherent in human existence, whereby a transformation and reordering of the body creates conditions for liberation from these conflicts.

Metaphoricity—the quality of a statement that has an indirect or mediated relationship to its referent. Metaphoricity is produced when the context (either immediately or culturally supplied) of a statement indicates that its significance is to be transferred from what is directly spoken of to an implied analogue.

Monachos—from the Greek word *monos*, "single," or "alone." *Monachos*, the monk, is therefore the solitary one. In the course of the fourth century in Christian tradition the term becomes a technical one in reference to many ascetic Christians who have chosen the way of withdrawal from everyday life. (See *Monastic Formation* below.)

Monastic Formation—systems employed to teach the monk the way of living in a monastery. These systems address every aspect of monastic living (daily schedule, eating habits, relationships, rules for prayer, reading, work). Special attention is given to discernment of spirits in monastic asceticism so that the nature of the demonic or angelic attack may be understood and appropriately addressed. (See *Monachos* above.)

Remnuoth—a label applied by Jerome to a third category of ascetics in Egypt he disparaged as heretical. Cassian referred to this same group as *sarabaitae*.

Social Body—the body of a person as it is understood from the perspective of the person's social attachments and relationships, as opposed to the perspective of the scientifically defined "atomic" body, separable from all social relationships. Since asceticism attempts to regulate both desire and social relationships, the social body becomes an important locus of ascetic activity.

Sōphrosynē—a Greek word most difficult to translate into English. Foucault describes this complex virtue as a "mode of relationship to self." As a male virtue, it was generally defined as moderation, self-mastery, or restraint. As a female virtue, it was generally understood as chastity.

SELECTED BIBLIOGRAPHY

The following list is designed to offer selected general and provocative guided reading for those interested in the intersection of historical, literary, rhetorical and discourse analysis, especially as applied to religious literature. It should complement the "Works Consulted" lists following each essay in this volume. For general reading suggestions on asceticism in particular, the reader is directed to W. Kaelber, "Asceticism," *Encyclopedia of Religion* (1987), ed. M. Eliade; Peter Brown's *Body and Society: Men, Women and Sexual Renunciation in Early Christianity* (1988), and to V. L. Wimbush, *Ascetic Behavior in Greco-Roman Antiquity: A Sourcebook* (1990).

Alter, R., and F. Kermode, eds.
    1987   *The Literary Guide to the Bible.* London: Collins.

Atkinson, C. W., et al., eds.
    1985   *Immaculate and Powerful: The Female in Sacred Image and Social Reality.* Boston: Beacon.

Auerbach, Erich
    1965   *Literary Language and Its Public in Late Antiquity and in the Middle Ages.* Trans. R. Mannheim. New York: Pantheon.

Bloch, M., ed.
    1975   *Political Language and Oratory in Traditional Society.* London: Academic.

Booth, W.
    1961   *The Rhetoric of Fiction.* Chicago: University of Chicago Press.

Burke, K.
    1962   *The Rhetoric of Religion.* Berkeley and Los Angeles: University of California Press.

Cameron, A.
    1991   *Christianity and the Rhetoric of Empire: The Development of Christian Discourse.* Sather Classical Lectures 55. Berkeley and Los Angeles: University of California Press.

Castelli, E.
    1991   *Imitating Paul: A Discourse of Power.* Louisville: Westminster/John Knox.

Conte, G. B.
1986   *The Rhetoric of Imitation*. Ithaca NY: Cornell University Press.

Eagleton, T.
1991   *Ideology*. London: Verso.

Foucault, M.
1972   *The Archaeology of Knowledge*. Trans. A. Sheridan-Smith. New York: Harper & Row.

Fowler, R., et al.
1979   *Language and Control*. London: Routledge & Kegan Paul.

Frye, N.
1982   *The Great Code: The Bible and Literature*. London: Routledge & Kegan Paul.

Gager, J.
1975   *The Social World of Early Christianity*. Englewood Cliffs NJ: Prentice-Hall.

Geertz, C.
1975   *The Interpretation of Cultures*. London: Hutchinson.

Gunn, G.
1979   *The Interpretation of Otherness: Literature, Religion, and the American Imagination*. New York: Oxford University Press.

Harpham, G.
1987   *The Ascetic Imperative in Culture and Criticism*. Chicago: University of Chicago Press.

Hobsbawn, E., and T. Ranger, eds.
1983   *The Invention of Tradition*. Cambridge: Cambridge University Press.

Hodge, R., and G. Kress.
1988   *Social Semiotics*. Cambridge: Polity.

Kennedy, G.
1972   *The Art of Rhetoric in the Roman World, 300 B.C.—A.D. 300*. Princeton: Princeton University Press.
1983   *Greek Rhetoric Under Christian Emperors*. Princeton: Princeton University Press.

Kermode, F.
: 1979 *The Genesis of Secrecy: On the Interpretation of Narrative.* Cambridge MA: Harvard University Press.

LaCapra, D.
: 1985 *History and Criticism.* Ithaca NY: Cornell University Press.

Laeuchli, S.
: 1965 *The Language of Faith.* London: Epworth.

McClendon, J. W., Jr.
: 1974 *Biography as Theology.* Nashville: Abingdon.

Man, Paul de.
: 1979 *Allegories of Reading.* New Haven: Yale University Press.

Mann, M.
: 1986 *Sources of Social Power: A History of Power from the Beginning to A.D. 1760.* Vol.1. Cambridge: Cambridge University Press.

Merrill, Robert, ed.
: 1988 *Ethics/Aesthetics: Post-Modern Positions.* Washington, D.C.: Maisonneuve.

Moretti, F.
: 1988 *Signs Taken for Wonders: Essays in the Sociology of Literary Forms.* Trans. S. Fischer, D. Forcas and D. Miller. London: Verso.

Ong, W.
: 1982 *Orality and Literacy: The Technologizing of the Word.* London: Methuen.

Ricoeur, P.
: 1977 *The Rule of Metaphor.* Trans. R. Czerny et al. Toronto: University of Toronto Press.
: 1981 *Hermeneutics and the Human Sciences: Essays on Language, Action and Interpretation.* Ed. and trans. J. B. Thompson. Cambridge: Cambridge University Press.

Said, E.
: 1983 *The World, The Text, and the Critic.* Cambridge MA: Harvard University Press.

Ste. Croix, G. E. M. de.
: 1981 *The Class Struggle in the Ancient Greek World.* London: Duckworth.

Soskice, J. M.
 1985   *Metaphor and Religious Language.* Oxford: Clarendon.

Sperber, D.
 1975   *Rethinking Symbolism.* Cambridge: Cambridge University Press.

Stock, B.
 1983   *The Implications of Literacy: Written Language and Models of Interpretation in the Eleventh and Twelfth Centuries.* Princeton: Princeton University Press.

Thompson, J. B.
 1990   *Ideology and Modern Culture.* Stanford CA: Stanford University Press.

White, H.
 1978   *Tropics of Discourse.* Baltimore: Johns Hopkins University Press.

www.ingramcontent.com/pod-product-compliance
Lightning Source LLC
Chambersburg PA
CBHW032259150426
43195CB00008BA/507